12/00

YA

920
H

Hill, Christine M.

Ten terrific au-
thors for teens

1200   20.95

DUE DATE

NoLex 1/13

Flint River R.L.S. - Peachtree

TEN TERRIFIC AUTHORS FOR TEENS

The *Collective Biographies* Series

Collective Biographies

TEN TERRIFIC AUTHORS FOR TEENS

Christine M. Hill

Enslow Publishers, Inc.

40 Industrial Road   PO Box 38
Box 398   Aldershot
Berkeley Heights, NJ 07922 Hants GU12 6BP
USA   UK

http://www.enslow.com

Library of Congress Cataloging-in-Publication Data

Hill, Christine M.
    Ten terrific authors for teens / Christine M. Hill.
        p. cm. — (Collective biographies)
    Includes bibliographical references and index.
    Contents: Judy Blume—Virginia Hamilton—Julius Lester—Lois Lowry—
Phyllis Reynolds Naylor—Katherine Paterson—Gary Paulsen—Gary Soto—
R.L. Stine—Laurence Yep.
    ISBN 0-7660-1380-4
    1. Authors, American—20th century—Biography—Juvenile literature.
    2. Young adult literature, American—History and criticism—Juvenile literature.
    3. Teenagers—Books and reading—Juvenile literature. [1. Authors, American.]
I. Title. II. Series.
PS490.H55 2000
810.9'9282—dc21
[B]
                                                      00-008008

Printed in the United States of America

10 9 8 7 6 5 4 3 2 1

To Our Readers:
All Internet addresses in this book were active and appropriate when we went to press.
Any comments or suggestions can be sent by e-mail to Comments@enslow.com or to
the address on the back cover.

Every effort has been made to locate all copyright holders of material used in this
book. If any errors or omissions have occurred, corrections will be made in future edi-
tions of this book.

Illustration Credits: Carolyn Soto, pp. 82, 89; Collection of Lois Lowry,
p. 45; Courtesy Houghton Mifflin, photo by Amanda Smith, p. 42;
Courtesy of R.L. Stine, p. 96; Courtesy of Random House Children's Books,
pp. 12, 72; Courtesy of Scholastic, by permission of Laurence Yep, p. 100;
Courtesy of Scholastic, with permission of R.L. Stine, p. 92; Enslow
Publishers, Inc., pp. 69, 80; Katherine Paterson, 63; Kathy Yep, p. 107;
Penguin Putnam Books for Young Readers, photo by Milan Sabatini, p. 38;
Photo by Milan Sabatini, p. 32; Phyllis Reynolds Naylor, p. 55; Ron Rovtar
photo courtesy of Virginia Hamilton, p. 22; Samantha Loomis Paterson, 60;
Simon and Schuster Children's Publishing Division (Katherine Lambert
Photography), p. 52; *The Horn Book*, p. 28; With permission of the
American Library Association, pp. 20, 78.

Cover Illustration: Ruth Wright Paulsen, Courtesy of Flannery Literary

Contents

Acknowledgment

Many thanks to the authors who reviewed their chapters and to those who contributed personal photographs.

Preface

How does a writer grow? Does he read avidly? Does he create his own books from early childhood? Does she love to listen to the storytellers in her family? Does she cast herself as the heroine of her own stories? Is he an excellent student? Or does he scarcely open a book, know nothing of stories, and barely graduate from high school? The ten writers in this book have done all these things. Their paths to success as writers for young people have been different. Yet they share common experiences.

All but two of them grew up surrounded by stories. Judy Blume, Lois Lowry, Phyllis Reynolds Naylor, Katherine Paterson, R. L. Stine, and Laurence Yep were read aloud to from an early age by their parents. Virginia Hamilton, Julius Lester, and Phyllis Reynolds Naylor sat spellbound as youngsters, listening to parents who were expert storytellers. Hamilton, Lester, and Blume also loved to eavesdrop on adult conversations, though they did not understand all the stories they heard. Only Gary Paulsen and Gary Soto, with their chaotic childhoods, missed out on hearing books or stories from a loving parent.

Paulsen and Soto, however, both connected with books in libraries as teenagers. Paulsen often credits the town librarian with giving him an identity through his library card. Reading provided the escape he needed from his miserable home life. Soto's father died young and his mother worked long hours. He has described his family as "pretty much . . . illiterate."[1] Yet, a chance encounter with a poetry book in his junior college library changed his life.

Most of the other writers haunted libraries as youngsters. Laurence Yep devoured science fiction at the San Francisco Public Library. Judy Blume so loved her library copy of the picture book *Madeline* that she hid it and told her mother it was lost. Virginia Hamilton won a prize from her school library for reading the most books. The Nashville, Tennessee, public library excluded African Americans when Julius Lester was growing up in that city. Still, every week he waited for the bookmobile to visit his neighborhood, so he could read his fill.

R. L. Stine could not get his favorite reading material at the library. He had to get it at the barber shop. Every Saturday, he read all the trashy horror comics he wanted without fear that his mother would take them away. It is not surprising that R. L. Stine created his own horror comics as a kid, but then so did Julius Lester! Phyllis Reynolds Naylor also created her own books as a child.

Katherine Paterson's mother cherished her daughter's first poem, published in a local newspaper when Katherine was only five. Naylor began selling stories to magazines when she was in high school. Yep sold his first story as a college student. Judy Blume and Lois Lowry did not write as children, but they did tell themselves stories. Each cast her own life as a great, continuing drama, with herself as the star.

Whatever the path each of these ten followed to writing, they have all achieved great honors. Virginia Hamilton and Katherine Paterson have received the Hans Christian Andersen Medal, world literature's highest honor for a young people's writer. Virginia Hamilton, Lois Lowry, Phyllis Reynolds Naylor, and Katherine Paterson have each won the Newbery Medal, for the best writing of the year in an American young people's book. Julius Lester, Gary Paulsen, and Laurence Yep have been runners-up for the Newbery. Judy Blume and Gary Paulsen have won the Margaret A. Edwards Award, for lifetime achievement by a young adult author. Gary Soto has won awards for poetry and young people's writing and for filmmaking. Only R. L. Stine has never won anything. But he can take consolation in being the best-selling young people's writer of all time.

It is fascinating to compare these accomplished writers, to see what hardships and sorrows they have overcome, to see what inspired them and what drives them. Though most of them began writing professionally decades ago, they are all still creating. They are writers through and through, and writers must write. As Gary Paulsen says, "I simply can't not write. . . . The hair goes up on the back of my neck when I work, even after 180 books."[2]

Judy Blume

1

Judy Blume

We can't move, thought nine-year-old Judy Sussman. This is Daddy's dangerous year.[1] Two of her father's brothers had died at age forty-two. Now he was forty-two himself. Mrs. Sussman and her two children, Judy and David, were going to move to Miami Beach for the winter of 1946–1947. David needed warm weather for his delicate health. Dr. Sussman would remain in New Jersey.

How could Judy keep her beloved father safe? She decided to make a deal with God. If God let her father live, she remembers promising, she would say "elaborate prayers . . . so many times a day, in just the right way."[2] Her father urged her not to let worry about him spoil the adventure of going to Florida.

When the school year ended in Miami Beach, Judy realized that she had enjoyed the best year of her life. Suddenly, she remembered that she had stopped praying for her father. Yet he had safely turned forty-three.

Judy Sussman was born in Elizabeth, New Jersey, on February 12, 1938. Her father, Dr. Rudolph Sussman, was a dentist. Her mother, Esther, was a homemaker who always wished she had become a teacher. Mrs. Sussman was a shy, silent worrier, while Dr. Sussman was talkative, outgoing, and a deep thinker.

Judy's brother, David, four years older, spent most of his time in his basement workshop. A brilliant loner who never liked school, he tinkered with electronic gadgets and his own inventions. "My brother did not please," Judy says. "So I was the child who had to please."[3] And she did. Judy earned top grades. Her mother boasted, "We never have to punish Judy . . . if you look at her wrong, she cries."[4]

Judy loved to hide and listen to adult conversations. To make sense of the confusing things she heard adults say, Judy made up stories about them. She invented stories while bouncing a ball against a wall, practicing piano, or playing paper dolls. She kept her imaginative life a secret.

By the time she became a teenager, she wanted to be exactly the same as everybody else. A late developer, she longed to have breasts and her period, like the other girls. "All I cared about was fitting in," Judy remembers.[5]

Girls ran the show at all-girl Battin High School. Judy joined the modern dance troupe, acted in plays, and wrote for the newspaper. She served as the features editor of the paper as a senior. She graduated with honors in 1956. She accepted her mother's advice about college: Find a husband, but get a teaching degree to fall back on.

During her junior year at New York University (NYU) in New York City, Judy became engaged to a young attorney, John Blume. A few weeks before the wedding, Judy's brother, David, and his pregnant wife flew back to New Jersey from Europe, where they lived. Dr. Sussman met them at the airport. He was about to become a grandfather and see his only daughter married. "What a banner year for our family," he exclaimed.[6] Only a few hours later, he suffered a heart attack. Judy held his hand and heard him whisper, "What lousy timing."[7] Minutes later, he died.

Jewish tradition holds that a death should not postpone a wedding. Judy's went on, as planned, in August 1959. It was a joyful occasion, as Dr. Sussman would have wished. But Judy's first year of marriage was marred by worry over her mother's suffering and by her own grief.

Judy Blume received her education degree from New York University in 1960, but she did not teach. The Blumes' daughter, Randy, was born in 1961 and their son, Larry, in 1963. Once her children entered nursery school, Blume began searching for a creative outlet. Of thirty families on their suburban New Jersey block, not one had a working mother. But Judy was no longer conforming. "I didn't fit in," she says.[8]

Blume registered for a course at NYU in writing for children. The instructor, children's author Lee Wyndham, was so encouraging that Blume took the course twice. When she sold her first story to a children's magazine, Wyndham presented her with a red rose in class.

In 1969, Blume's picture book *The One in the Middle Is the Green Kangaroo* was accepted for publication. When the letter arrived, Blume ran to her children's playroom. She began throwing their playthings all over the room with happiness. Larry's best friend ran home crying. "Larry's mother is crazy," she reported.[9]

The year 1970 saw the publication of her first two children's novels, *Iggie's House* and the book that made her famous, *Are You There God? It's Me, Margaret.* The character of Margaret Simon was written from Blume's own experience. She remembers everything she did and felt as a child with total recall. To this day, grown women who devoured the book as girls will respond to the title by chanting, "We must—we must—we must increase our bust," as Margaret and her friends do.[10]

Books poured out of Judy Blume in the 1970s: two in 1971; three in 1972; then one a year until 1975. The hyper-mischievous Fudge, in *Tales of a Fourth Grade Nothing*, was based on Larry Blume. Like Fudge, he dumped bowls of food over his head. Unlike Fudge, he never swallowed a turtle. "Although," his mother admits, "I'm sure that if we had a turtle, he would have eaten it."[11]

Blubber was based on what Blume remembers as a "terrible, terrible" case of bullying that Randy Blume witnessed in fifth grade. One girl in the class was singled out and persecuted by others. They actually put her on trial and found her guilty. "Guilty of what," Judy Blume demanded—powerlessness?[12]

Randy was also the source of the young adult novel *Forever*. She asked her mother to write a novel about teenagers who fall in love, have sex, and do not suffer as a result. *Blubber* and *Forever* are among Judy Blume's most frequently censored books. More than a hundred attempts have been made to remove them from schools and libraries. Blume believes that adults should discuss with their children the issues raised by her books. Censorship only saves adults "from having to answer their children's questions," she says.[13]

In 1975, Judy and John Blume divorced. She quickly remarried, to physicist Thomas Kitchens. She moved with him and her children, first to England, then to New Mexico.

Blume's most autobiographical novel, *Starring Sally J. Freedman As Herself,* was published in 1977. In it, Sally lives apart from her adored father for the winter in Miami Beach in 1947. To deal with her fears for her father's life and the deaths of her relatives in concentration camps during World War II, she makes up elaborate games in which she saves them. Unlike the fictional Sally, Blume did not lose close family members to the death camps.

By 1979, Blume's hasty second marriage was over. She and Kitchens had simply not known each other well enough when they married, she believed.[14] Blume and her children stayed in Santa Fe, New Mexico, so Larry could finish high school.

Blume considers *Tiger Eyes,* published in 1981, to be her best young adult novel. Its heroine, Davey Wexler, is paralyzed by fear after her father is murdered during a robbery. Blume admits that *Tiger Eyes* reflects her own feelings about her father's death.

For several years, Blume wondered whether she would ever "take another chance on love."[15] Then she met former law professor and nonfiction writer George Cooper. Their relationship blossomed and she moved back to New York City in 1985 to be with him. They married two years later.

Since the 1970s, Blume had received thousands of letters from children, describing their lives and problems. Often they asked her for help or advice. She decided to organize a collection of letters with her comments as a book for adults, so that they could communicate better with their children. After *Letters to Judy* was published in 1986, the letters actually increased. Blume began receiving several thousand letters a month, often about serious problems, such as sexual abuse. Trying to help so many letter writers "cost me a couple of years," she says. It was nearly "overwhelming."[16]

Blume has published far less in the 1990s. She devotes time to her Kids Fund Foundation, which promotes family communication, and works with the National Coalition Against Censorship. At her two vacation homes she enjoys summer, her favorite season, year-round. On Martha's Vineyard, Massachusetts, her numerous small boats are named after her book characters. In Key West, Florida, she bikes through town on a classic Schwinn like the one Sally J. Freedman rode.

Blume enjoys keeping in shape by working out at a gym. "It makes the creative juices flow," she finds.[17] Her current favorite sport is kayaking. She has, however, given up daily tap dancing, which she studied seriously for many years and still enjoys.

Son Larry Blume is a filmmaker whose work includes a dramatization of his mother's book *Otherwise Known As Sheila the Great.* Daughter Randy is a commercial airline pilot and a writer, too. Randy's adult novel about flying, *Crazy in the Cockpit*, was published in 1999.

Blume has never been a favorite of reviewers or award committees. She was surprised to be selected

Judy Blume, third from left, is congratulated by members of the American Library Association committee that named her an outstanding writer for teens.

by the American Library Association in 1996 for the Margaret A. Edwards Award, which honors outstanding contribution to literature for young adults.[18] Millions of readers, not numerous awards, have made her one of the best-selling young people's novelists of all time. "In certain important ways," journalist and fan Ellen Barry says, "she raised us all."[19]

Virginia Hamilton

2

Virginia Hamilton

Every year, Levi Perry gathered his ten children around him. "[Sit] down," he would say. "And I will tell you about slavery and why I ran, so that it will never happen to you."[1] Perry was a child in 1857 when he escaped from slavery with the help of the Underground Railroad, a secret network of people who helped slaves flee to freedom. Virginia Hamilton's mother, Etta Belle, was one of the children at Levi Perry's knee. She named her youngest daughter Virginia, after the state Perry fled. That way Virginia Hamilton, too, would always remember.

A Yellow Springs, Ohio, farm had been home to Virginia Hamilton's ancestors for generations when she was born there on March 12, 1936. Virginia, her two brothers, two sisters, and many cousins could roam and play all day long and never leave family land. Her mother made only three rules for Virginia during childhood: Attend Sunday school, make the honor roll, and come home before dark.

Virginia grew up surrounded by books and stories. Her father, Kenneth Hamilton, the dining service manager at Antioch College, owned an extensive library. He subscribed to intellectual magazines like *The New Yorker* and *The Crisis.* He was the one with "the knowledge," Virginia remembers.[2] Etta Belle Hamilton was the skillful storyteller. She could take a family anecdote and "polish it to a saga," says her daughter.[3] From her mother, Virginia learned the shape of a good story.

Virginia wrote from an early age. She kept a notebook and filled it with things that she heard adults discussing but that she did not understand. "I figured someday I would know what they were talking about," she says.[4] She also used it to describe "the pictures in my head."[5]

After high school in Yellow Springs, Virginia attended Antioch College and then Ohio State University. Already, though, the writer's life in New York City was calling her. For a while, she divided her time between college and the city. In 1958, she moved to New York permanently.

Hamilton took a series of part-time jobs to give herself time to write. She sang with a jazz band for a while. At a party for musician Charles Mingus, she met the jazz great's manager, Arnold Adoff. In addition to managing Mingus, the Jewish, Bronx-born Adoff wrote poetry and taught school. Hamilton and Adoff fell in love and married in 1960.

Around this time, Hamilton ran into an old college friend, Janet Schulman, who now worked for a children's publisher. What happened to the stories Hamilton used to write in college? They might make interesting children's books, Schulman suggested. Hamilton had not read a children's book since her own childhood. What would one be like? she wondered.[6] Hamilton found an editor who recognized her talent and agreed to work with her.

The newlyweds moved to Europe. They lived in France and in Spain, Hamilton's longtime dream. While there, she labored over her children's novel. Then, when the civil rights movement exploded in the United States in the early 1960s, the couple returned home to give their support. Their children were born in New York City. A daughter, Leigh, came along in 1963 and a son, Jaime Levi, in 1967.

Hamilton's first book, *Zeely*, was published in 1967. Developed from her college stories, it tells of a girl and her brother who visit their uncle in the country for the summer. When they see a tall, ebony-skinned hog-farmer's daughter there, they imagine she is a Watusi queen. Critics today view *Zeely* as the turning-point book for the depiction of African Americans in young people's literature. "It is difficult to underestimate . . . the importance it had in its own day for encouraging other black writers to speak for the black child," wrote one critic.[7] Prior to *Zeely*, in children's literature nearly all fictional portraits of blacks had been written by whites.

The House of Dies Drear, published in 1968, won the Edgar Allan Poe Award for best children's mystery of the year. In it, Hamilton reached back to her childhood for characters and situations, as she would again and again. The many Underground Railroad stations in the Yellow Springs area, with their hidden rooms and tunnels, inspired Drear House. Hamilton had a niece who rode farm horses bareback in her pajamas at twilight. "That's Pesty," she says, identifying one of the book's characters.[8]

By 1969, the Hamilton-Adoff family had had enough of New York. "I loved the City until the moment I could no longer stand it," remembers Hamilton.[9] She found she needed quiet and less stimulation to write. She wanted to see green again. She and Adoff bought two acres of Perry family land in Ohio. They built a modern, redwood house with no windows, only skylights and sliding glass doors. Hamilton called it her "castle."[10]

By this time, Adoff had become a professional young people's writer himself. He had grown frustrated, as a New York public school teacher, trying to find books to mirror his African-American students' lives. He gathered poems by African-American writers into an anthology, *I Am the Darker Brother*, in 1968.

Many books of his own writing, both poetry and prose, have followed.

Hamilton won a Newbery Honor award for *The Planet of Junior Brown* in 1971. She had conceived the idea for this book in New York, while playing in the park with her daughter. Hamilton observed a number of children obviously playing hooky from school. She saw one of the boys take apart a complicated toy. Why is such a smart child not in school? she wondered. This became the seed for the society of homeless boys caring for one another in *The Planet of Junior Brown.*[11]

In 1974, Hamilton became the first African American to be awarded the Newbery Medal. *M. C. Higgins the Great,* the winning book, tells the story of a boy trying to save his family home from being buried by a pile of coal mining waste looming on the mountain above it. Hamilton brought her husband and children to the award ceremony. She and her eight-year-old son peeked into the hall where dinner would be served. Jaime eyed the handsomely dressed waiters and sparkling table settings with amazement. "Wow, Mom," he exclaimed, "you never told me *this* is what you'd been doing!"[12] The award boosted the book's sales so much that Hamilton was able to build a "Newbery" swimming pool.[13]

Sweet Whispers, Brother Rush was named Hamilton's second Newbery Honor Book in 1983. It is the story of an abused young woman, caring for her gravely ill brother, who sees and falls in love with

Virginia Hamilton with husband Arnold Adoff, daughter Leigh, and son Jaime.

a ghost. Writing it "put to rest" the emotions Hamilton still felt from a childhood experience of believing she had seen a ghost.[14]

Willie Bea and the Time the Martians Landed (1983) drew more heavily on Perry family lore than any of her other books. On Halloween in 1938, a radio play version of the H. G. Wells science fiction novel *The War of the Worlds* was broadcast. Like thousands of other Americans, the Perrys did not realize at first that it was a play. They believed that the Martians were really invading. While some family members cowered in the basement, Hamilton's aunt led the men on a search for Martians. Armed with shotguns, they blasted anything that moved in the sky. Hamilton also remembers walking across the narrow beam at the top of her family's barn, the way her character Willie Bea does.

Hamilton won a third Newbery Honor for *In the Beginning* in 1989. In it, Hamilton retold creation stories from religions and cultures around the world. In addition to folklore, Hamilton has tried her hand at history and biography over the years as well.

Honor followed honor for Hamilton in the 1990s. In 1992, she became only the fifth American to receive the Hans Christian Andersen Medal from the International Board on Books for Young People. This is the highest award in young people's literature, established in 1956 for worldwide achievement. The American Library Association gave her the Laura Ingalls Wilder Award for lifetime achievement in

1995. The same year, she was named a fellow by the John D. and Catherine T. MacArthur Foundation. Called a "Genius Grant," this prestigious award honors outstanding creativity and provides the fellows with an income for five years so they can concentrate on their work. Hamilton is the only young people's writer ever to receive it.

Hamilton's children both attended Ohio State University, like their mother, and both studied music. Leigh is an opera singer. Although Leigh's father grew up in an opera-loving family, her mother knows nothing about it. "I'm sure that's why she chose it!" says Hamilton.[15] Jaime is a songwriter with a band that performs in the New York City area and has released a CD. Hamilton describes her son's style as "soulful acoustic alternative rock."[16]

In 1998, Hamilton noted that she had published more than a book a year for thirty-one years. She was ready to slow down a little, to garden more and travel less. Her husband, she observed playfully, was trying to teach her how to nap. He had instructed her to lie down on a comfortable couch and close her eyes. Impossible, she responded. "I at once recall something I hadn't done and jump right up again." People like her "breathe, dream, dance and sing writing," she says.[17] She never intends to quit.

3

Julius Lester

Little Julius Lester waited at the end of the dirt road. He strained for a sight of his father's big blue Plymouth. Reverend Lester would soon be paying his weekly visit to his wife and son. While Reverend Lester taught at a summer school for ministers, Julius and his mother stayed with relatives. Julius missed his father.[1] But Reverend Lester's visit also meant that the family would be able to go to town in his car and shop. Reverend Lester had forbidden his wife and son to ride the segregated buses of Arkansas in the 1940s.

The next day, Julius and his parents rode down Pine Bluff's main street. Julius noticed a big, round clock in a store window. When he spied the name

Julius Lester

over the clock—A-L-T-S-C-H-U-L—he exclaimed, "Momma, that is the name on Grandmomma's mailbox!" Silence filled the car, then Reverend Lester explained that it was Julius's great-grandfather's name. The people who owned the store were his cousins. Adolf Altschul came from Germany and fell in love with Maggie Carson, who was newly freed from slavery. Julius's great-grandfather was a white man, a Jew.[2]

Julius quietly turned this information over in his mind. He did not know what it meant, but it made him feel different. It left him with "wonder and questions," he said later.[3]

Julius Lester was born on January 27, 1939. His parents were in their forties. Their older son, Woodie Daniel, Jr., was nine years old. Reverend Lester was pastor of a church in Saint Louis, Missouri, at the time.

The Reverend W. D. Lester, Sr., had been orphaned as a teenager. He raised his younger brothers while working his way through college and the seminary. His son Julius calls him "an American success story" who carried himself with great seriousness and dignity.[4] He was also the more tender parent. Lester remembers his father spooning sugar into a glass of milk to persuade Julius to drink it. He was the one who always nursed Julius through illness. Julius's mother, Julia, after whom he was named, was silent and stern. "She had to prepare me to survive," Lester says.[5]

Reverend Lester became pastor at a new church in Kansas City, Kansas, when Julius was two. Then, in 1953, when Julius was fourteen, his father was appointed an administrator of the Methodist Church. He was one of its few African-American officials. The Lesters moved to Nashville, Tennessee, "the country of NO COLORED ALLOWED," as Lester calls the Deep South of those days.[6]

The African-American community cherished its exceptional children, "the carrier[s] of dreams," Lester remembers. He often heard people predict that he would be somebody important someday.[7] Julius was an outstanding student who graduated from high school a year early. He played several musical instruments, wrote and illustrated his own horror comics, and excelled at chess. He also read avidly. In books he discovered a world beyond "the segregated world I was forced to live in," a world of "dreams and possibilities."[8]

At Fisk University, in Nashville, Lester began a spiritual quest that would last several decades. He studied and explored Roman Catholicism and Eastern and Native American religions. He rejected the Christianity of his boyhood but attended church to avoid embarrassing his minister father. In return, Reverend Lester kept "his hands off my soul," his son says. "I will always respect him for that."[9]

Lester graduated from Fisk in 1960 with a bachelor's degree. He moved to New York City the following year and worked at a variety of jobs. He achieved some success as a folk singer, recording two albums of his own songs and traditional music. He married a researcher named Joan Steinau in 1962. They soon had two children, Jody and Malcolm.

Lester began to write articles for the music press. He also began to write political commentary, particularly about the growing civil rights movement. He often sang at benefits to raise funds for the Student Nonviolent Coordinating Committee (SNCC), a civil rights group.

In the summer of 1964, Lester traveled to Mississippi to sing at SNCC voter registration rallies. One hot day, he stood at the edge of a great field near Laurel, Mississippi. Suddenly, he was gripped by a strong feeling. A hundred years before, he thought, a slave stood here looking out just as I am. Perhaps it had even been his ancestor, since his father's family had been enslaved in the same state. A question possessed him. "What was it like to be a slave . . . what did that slave feel?"[10]

Lester went to work full-time for SNCC as head of the photography department. He began to travel with Stokely Carmichael, the organization's militant new chairman. Carmichael and his supporters had recently expelled all the white members from SNCC. Lester and Carmichael visited Cuba, espousing the slogan "Black Power," which Carmichael had made famous. Lester also traveled to North Vietnam.

In 1968, Lester published a history of black militant movements, written for adults. His editor remarked that his style was really very simple. Had Lester ever considered writing for young people? she wondered. At a meeting with the publisher's head of children's books, Lester remembered his inspiring moment in Mississippi. He wanted to write about what it was like to be enslaved, he told her.[11]

Lester wove together the voices of slavery survivors, which he had gleaned from archives at the Library of Congress and elsewhere. He chose those voices that "hit me in the gut," he said.[12] He tied the testimony together with his own chillingly matter-of-fact narrative. The work "came easily," he remembers. "It was clear to me that writing this book was one of the things I had been put on earth to do."[13] *To Be a Slave* was published in 1969. It was named a Newbery Honor Book by the American Library Association. Lester was only the second African-American author to win this award. Arna Bontemps was the first, in 1948.

Lester had begun hosting a radio talk show in New York City. During 1968 and 1969, conflict over community control of public schools rocked the city. Tensions heightened in many neighborhoods where the teachers were mostly Jewish and the students mostly African American. On one program highlighting the issue, a Lester guest read poetry that was widely believed to be anti-Jewish. On a later show, one guest made anti-Semitic remarks. Some people accused Lester himself of anti-Semitism. He denied it.

Julius and Joan Lester divorced in 1970. He moved to Amherst, Massachusetts, to do research and teach in the Afro-American Studies department of the University of Massachusetts. His son, Malcolm, came to live with him in 1975. Eventually, his ex-wife and daughter settled nearby as well.

During the seventies, Lester wrote several volumes of historical fiction for young adults. *Two Love Stories* and *Long Journey Home*, both published in 1972, were based on true stories of the Reconstruction period after the Civil War. *Long Journey Home* was a runner-up for the National Book Award.

Lester divided his time between writing for adults and for young people. Writing for children gave him the pleasure of "just, straight, tell[ing] a story," he says.[14] In some ways, he actually found writing for young people more rewarding. "I like the audience and the responses I get," he admitted.[15] He was also concerned about the lack of books about African Americans available for young people. He wrote to supply them for children like his own.

Lester remarried in 1979. His new wife, Alida Fechner, had a young daughter, Elena. The Lesters' son, David, was born later that year.

Meanwhile, Lester continued to struggle with his religious beliefs. A course he taught on the history of Black/Jewish relations led him to learn about the Holocaust and the Jewish religion. The more he

Lester has written for adults, but he prefers writing for young readers. "I like the audience and the responses I get," he says.

knew, the greater affinity he felt for the Jewish people.

One night, shortly after the death of his father in 1981, Lester had a vision. He saw himself dancing, twirling, arms extended in praise of God. He wore a yarmulke, the Jewish skullcap. "I want to get out of bed and dance," he thought. "I want to shout: I am a Jew! I am a Jew!"[16]

Lester began to study Judaism and the Hebrew language. In 1982, he converted to Judaism. His wife and younger son converted three years later.

Lester's autobiography, *Lovesong*, published in 1988, chronicles his spiritual journey. It eloquently describes the joy he takes in practicing the religion of his great-grandfather. He reveals that he found his Altschul cousins, so long after wondering about them as a boy. Ironically, they had all become Christians. "I am the only Jew left in the family," he marvels.[17]

In addition to his young adult novels, Lester's specialty as a children's writer has been retelling folktales from the African and African-American traditions. His frequent collaborations with award-winning illustrator Jerry Pinkney have been published throughout the eighties and nineties. Lester attributes his flair for folklore to his father, who loved traditional stories and also told stories as a preacher.

Lester loves movies and music of all kinds. Leading musical prayer at his synagogue gives him particular pride. He now serves as lay religious leader of a synagogue in Vermont. He collects cookbooks and is a skilled cook. When he began keeping a kosher kitchen, he relished the opportunity to try a variety of kosher recipes from around the world. He bakes the Sabbath bread himself every week.

Lester and Alida Fechner divorced in 1991. In 1995, he married a third time. His new wife, Milan Sabatini, has a daughter, Lian. Now in his sixties, Lester believes he is entering a "powerfully creative time. . . . I have more ideas than I can use," he says. After years of personal turmoil, he has found happiness. "There is so much inside of me I want to come out and now is the time."[18]

4

Lois Lowry

Four-year-old Lois pulled on her father's Army-major cap over her blond curls. Lois did not care that it clashed with her pink flowered pajamas. She loved to wear that cap and march around like a soldier. Her father laughed and laughed, then snapped her picture, calling her "the best show in town."[1]

Robert Hammersberg, a career Army dentist, and his wife, Katherine, were stationed in Honolulu, Hawaii, when Lois was born on March 20, 1937. They already had a three-year-old daughter, Helen. Like most military families, they moved frequently. In 1939, they were transferred to New York. Not long after, World War II broke out and Dr. Hammersberg

Lois Lowry

was sent abroad. Lois would not live with him again for eight years.

Mrs. Hammersberg wanted to be close to her own family during the war. She moved with her daughters to rural Carlisle, Pennsylvania, where she had grown up. Carlisle is a small college town in the central part of the state. Lois's brother, Jon, was born shortly after they arrived.

Lois Lowry admits that she stood apart from the children in her school and neighborhood. "I was a solitary child who lived in the world of books and my own imagination," she says.[2] She entered first grade already reading. Though no one had taught her, she had puzzled out the meanings of the letters and sounds herself at age three. At the end of first grade, school officials skipped her to third grade. Lois was delighted to plunge into chapter books, but shocked that she was expected to multiply and divide. She had barely learned addition and subtraction.

The Hammersberg family reunited in Japan in 1948. They lived in a military housing compound called Washington Heights. It resembled a perfect, miniature American town set inside, but isolated from, the Japanese city of Tokyo. Lois and her best friend hopped on their bikes at every opportunity to explore the city streets outside the compound. They watched the Japanese children in their navy blue school uniforms but were too shy to speak to them.

Dr. Hammersberg stayed behind when the rest of the family returned to the United States in 1950. Finally, he joined them permanently when he was posted to a military base in New York City.

Lois spent most of her high school years at the Packer Collegiate Institute, an elite private girls' school in Brooklyn. By then, she knew she wanted to be a writer. A poem she wrote won a national prize for teens.

One day, Lois decided to experiment with changing her identity. She shed her boring real name when she made a hairdresser's appointment. Her name was Cynthia Randolph, she told the woman on the phone. Unexpectedly, her mother accompanied Lois to the salon. "Cynthia," the receptionist called to them. Lois rose and went in. She remembers her mother looking "half puzzled, half amused," but not saying a word.[3]

Lois graduated at the top of her class in 1954. The caption under her yearbook picture read "future novelist." On a scholarship, she attended Pembroke College at Brown University, noted for its writing program. Lois now regrets that she did not value college more. Like most of her friends there in the 1950s, she was more concerned with finding a husband than with her education. She now marvels that though she distinctly remembers which of her friends were engaged or going steady, she does not know what any of them studied or wanted to be.[4]

By the time she was a teenager, Lois knew she wanted to be a writer.

Lois dropped out of college after two years to marry Donald Grey Lowry in 1956. Her husband was a navy officer whose career took them to four different postings in four years. After his discharge, they moved to Cambridge, Massachusetts, so he could attend law school. By the time she was twenty-six, Lois Lowry had four children: Alix, born in 1958; Grey, 1959; Kristin, 1961; and Benjamin, 1962.

The Lowrys settled near Portland, Maine, where Donald Lowry began practicing law. They had a big house with lots of land and pets. As her children grew up, "so did I," Lois Lowry says.[5] She returned to college part-time, graduating from the University of Southern Maine in 1972. Then she enrolled in graduate school and also studied photography on the side.

Lowry began selling articles and short stories to magazines, often illustrating them with her own photographs. One article, which appeared in *The New York Times*, chronicled her appearance on the television quiz show *Jeopardy*. She lost. For weeks afterward, her son would look sadly at her and shake his head to think of her wrong answer to the final Jeopardy question. How could anyone know so little about baseball? he wondered.[6]

Meanwhile, an editor at Houghton Mifflin Company, who admired one of Lowry's published short stories, asked her if she had ever considered writing for young people. This interested Lowry. She wrote a story about two teenage sisters in conflict. She based it on her relationship with her own sister, Helen, who had died of cancer at age twenty-eight. *A Summer to Die* was emotionally "accurate to my own life," she says.[7] Critics praised it highly when it was published in 1977.

The same year, she and Donald Lowry divorced. When she married as a teenager, "I had pretended to be—maybe I was" a conventional wife and homemaker, she says. Later "I turned out to be somebody else entirely. Fortunately my kids like me anyway."[8]

In 1979, Lowry published the first book in her series about the Krupnik family, *Anastasia Krupnik*. The series would make her one of America's most popular young people's writers. She modeled Anastasia on Amy Carter, daughter of U.S. president Jimmy Carter, as well as on her own daughters. Kristin Lowry actually once answered her mother's fan mail, as Anastasia answers her father's in the book series. Kristin's answers, however, were "not quite as silly," Lowry admits.[9] Lowry has published nine Anastasia books and three about Anastasia's brother Sam.

Autumn Street, also published in 1979, remains one of Lowry's favorites. Based on her Carlisle childhood, almost all its characters were real people she grew up with. One of the people Lowry gave a copy to was her grandparents' cook, a character in the book. At age ninety-five, the retired cook still lived in Carlisle.

Around this time, Lowry went on a date with a man named Martin Small. While they talked over coffee, Small remarked, "You have good ideas, Cornelius. When I am king I will give you a green hat."[10] Lowry feared she was out with a very strange person, but he reassured her. He was quoting a line from a children's story about Babar, the elephant. Lowry believed that a fifty-year-old man who knew a picture book by heart must be a great guy. They have shared each other's lives ever since.

In 1988, Lowry vacationed with a longtime friend, Annelise Platt. On the Bermuda beach, they talked about growing up. Until then, Lowry had never realized how much her friend's childhood in Denmark had been affected by the Nazi conquest of her country during World War II. Platt's memories inspired Lowry to write *Number the Stars*, which won the 1990 Newbery Medal. It is the story of two friends, one Christian, one Jewish, and Denmark's heroic rescue of its Jewish citizens from certain death at Nazi hands.

Many people have wondered what inspired *The Giver*, published in 1993 and winner of the Newbery Medal in 1994. In the acceptance speech for her second Newbery, Lowry described the many "streams" from her life and experiences that fed the "river" of this powerful book.[11] Her greatest inspiration was her parents' last days. Both of them were frail and were being cared for in a nursing home. Her mother was ill and nearly blind, but she vividly remembered her life and loved to talk about it. Her father's health was much better, but he could barely remember his children. When Lowry visited them, she was struck that one parent "had released all his memories and lost them" while the other "still continued all those stories and memories."[12]

In *The Giver*, set some time in the future, a young boy, Jonas, is chosen to receive all the memories of his society, which thoroughly regulates people's lives in a way it considers perfect. When those memories become his, Jonas realizes that he must escape its false perfection. Lowry will not say more about *The Giver*'s ambiguous ending, preferring readers to consider it for themselves. However, she has said that she feels it is an optimistic ending and that Jonas and the baby he kidnaps will live.[13]

Lowry and Martin Small live in Cambridge, Massachusetts. They have a country home in New Hampshire, where Lowry enjoys gardening. They travel all over the world. Lowry is a great reader and movie buff. Her older daughter, Alix, a computer specialist, is battling multiple sclerosis. Kristin lives in Maine with her son, James. Lowry's younger son, Benjamin, a lawyer, had a brief career as a minor-league baseball player.

Grey, a navy pilot, died in a plane crash in 1995. His two-year-old daughter, Nadine, said that "Papa went to heaven in his airplane." He's there with Santa

Claus, she decided.[14] Lowry's grief led her to collect her own memories in a photographic autobiography, *Looking Back*, published in 1998. As we share our memories, whether in books or within our families, Lowry believes, we all become Givers.[15]

Phyllis Reynolds Naylor

"Make up a story!" the kindergarten teacher called to her students. She sat on the floor and invited them to come to her with their ideas. Little Phyllis Reynolds hurried over for a chance to dictate her story. The teacher wrote it down and gave it to her. Other kindergartners took turns, but Phyllis joined the line again and again. Finally, the teacher insisted that Phyllis stop telling stories. She had taken "quite enough turns for one day."[1]

Phyllis came from a family of storytellers. Both of her parents read aloud to their children from the family's small but treasured book collection. Her father, Eugene Reynolds, entertained Phyllis, her older sister, Norma, and younger brother, John, with

Phyllis Reynolds Naylor

tales of his southern boyhood. Their mother, Lura Reynolds, invented more fanciful stories, like those about the continuing antics of a kitten named Fluffy.

Phyllis Dean Reynolds was born in Anderson, Indiana, on January 4, 1933. The Reynolds family lived in eight different midwestern communities as she grew up. Each time they moved, it was to find better employment for Mr. Reynolds, a traveling salesman. The poor economy had forced Mr. Reynolds to drop out of college and give up his dream of becoming a minister. This period of the 1930s, called the Great Depression, was one of high unemployment and financial hardship for most Americans.

When ten-year-old Phyllis began to construct her own books, the family still did not have much money. She was permitted to play only with paper that had been used on one side. Every day, she scavenged the most presentable sheets from the house's wastebaskets. These she stapled into little books, filling them with stories and pictures. Sometimes she pasted a colored strip over the stapled edge and added a pocket made from a used envelope. "I was the author, illustrator, printer, binder and librarian all in one," she says.[2]

The Reynolds family settled in Joliet, Illinois, for Phyllis's junior high and high school years. At Joliet Township High School, she sang in choral groups and acted in plays and musicals. She continued writing, both for school and for pleasure.

One day, Phyllis received a letter from a former Sunday school teacher. The teacher now edited a religious newspaper for children and remembered Phyllis's love of telling stories. If Phyllis could write something good enough, the teacher would publish it. Phyllis promptly wrote a story about an injured baseball player and received a check for $4.67 by return mail. At sixteen, Phyllis became a published writer. This was easy, she thought. "What a life!"[3]

The teacher published quite a few of Phyllis's stories and poems. Soon Phyllis began submitting manuscripts to the magazines she saw in stores, like *Jack and Jill* and *Seventeen*. For two years, she received nothing but rejections. "[I was] terribly embarrassed," she remembered.[4] What had been good enough for a Sunday school paper had not been professional quality writing. Just about to give up, she took heart when she found an acceptance letter in her mail, along with a $60 check.

In 1951, eighteen-year-old Phyllis graduated from high school. Almost immediately, she married a twenty-five-year-old graduate student she had dated for a year. Her life was about to become quite different.

In *Crazy Love*, an adult book she wrote about this disastrous marriage, she calls her husband "Ted Moreno." The first three years of their relationship seemed normal. Phyllis attended and graduated from Joliet Junior College. Her brilliant and cultured

During high school, Phyllis dreamed of being published. But for two years, all the stories she sent to *Seventeen* and other magazines were rejected.

husband introduced her to literature, theater, and classical music.

When "Moreno" went to graduate school at the University of Chicago, Phyllis took a job as a hospital secretary to support them. Suddenly, he began to show signs of mental illness. He dropped out of graduate school and the couple traveled the Midwest. During this time, Phyllis's magazine writing provided most of their meager income. None of the psychiatric treatment he received seemed to help. At last, after "Moreno" was committed to a state hospital, the two divorced.

While waiting for her divorce to become final, Phyllis lived in Maryland and worked as an editorial assistant. There she met speech pathologist Rex Naylor and they fell in love. Their marriage in 1960 was "one of the best decisions of my life," she says.[5]

Phyllis and Rex Naylor settled in Bethesda, Maryland. Their sons, Jeffrey and Michael, were born in the 1960s. When her older boy was just a baby, Phyllis Naylor finished college. She graduated from American University in 1963 with a degree in psychology.

While raising preschoolers, Naylor continued to be a successful magazine writer. She had paid her college tuition with her writing income. The prospect of writing a novel "frightened me" though, she says.[6] She worried that she would get bored writing about the same characters for a year or more. Instead, Naylor collected her best magazine stories for kids in a book called *The Galloping Goat and Other Stories.* It was published in 1965, followed by *Grasshoppers in the Soup,* a volume of her best stories for teens.

Finally, she felt ready to tackle a novel. Naylor set *What the Gulls Were Singing* in a seaside boarding-house and filled it with every adventure she thought kids might possibly enjoy. It was a "mess," she now admits.[7] The first editor who rejected it still saw Naylor's talent. If Naylor would completely rewrite the book, the editor said, she would consider it again. Naylor took the editor's advice, and the book was published in 1967.

Since then, Naylor has written two to three books a year, totaling more than one hundred. "Writing is as necessary for her as eating or sleeping," her husband says, adding that she "organizes her waking hours like a railroad timetable."[8] When her sons were small, knowing that they would be home from school in six hours was a powerful writing motivator. Now that they are grown, she motivates herself. Naylor spends up to ten hours a day writing, revising, planning, and doing writing-related correspondence.

Like many authors, Naylor is often asked how she gets her ideas. "[From] absolutely everything that ever happened to me, all mixed up with whatever happened to anybody else, all mixed up with imaginings," she replies.[9]

Naylor's popular Alice McKinley series was inspired by "many of the embarrassing things that happened to me as a young girl," she says.[10] Though she never stuck crayons in her nostrils and shook her head like an elephant, as Alice does, she saw a classmate do it in third grade. "[That is] the stupidest thing I have ever seen in my life," she thought.[11] The Tarzan scene in *The Agony of Alice* did happen to her, however. "Don't ask," Naylor warns. She thoroughly enjoys writing the Alice books, which started in 1985 and numbered twelve by 2000. She intends to continue writing one book a year for the series until the fictional Alice turns eighteen.[12]

In 1990, the Naylors visited friends in Shiloh, West Virginia. On a hike, they spotted a thin and frightened beagle who followed them down the trail. When Phyllis Naylor whistled to the dog, it "bounded over, leaping up to lick my cheek," she says.[13] But the Naylors could not adopt the stray. Neither could their friends, the Maddens, who told them that pets were constantly abandoned in the nearby hills.

The dog's plight gripped Naylor. She returned home to write, she said, "at breakneck speed," the story of Marty Preston, a boy who wrestles with his conscience over the fate of an abused dog named Shiloh.[14] While working on the book, Naylor heard good news. The Maddens had met the dog again and changed their minds. They adopted the stray, a female, whom they named Clover.

Shiloh won the 1991 Newbery Medal. "Thank you for loving Marty Preston and his dog as much as I do," Naylor told the librarians at the awards ceremony.[15] Two sequels followed: *Shiloh Season*, in 1996, and *Saving Shiloh*, in 1997.

"What spare time?" Naylor asks in response to a question about what she does in her spare time.[16] Still, she does admit to enjoying the theater, snorkeling, and preparing a big, traditional Christmas. Writing remains her "addiction" though, she says. "Once the thrill of putting words on paper had a hold on me, the magic never left."[17]

Katherine Paterson

6

Katherine Paterson

"If you were born in China, how come you're not Chinese?" Katherine was asked this so many times as a child, she developed a snappy answer. "If a cat is born in a garage," she would retort, "does that make it an automobile?"[1]

Katherine spoke Chinese before she spoke English. Her parents, George and Mary Womeldorf, were missionaries when she was born on October 31, 1932, in Qing Jiang, China. They preached Christianity and did social work among the Chinese people. But civil war swept China in the 1930s. One political group battled another and then the Japanese invaded. Katherine's parents could not do their missionary work in the middle of a war. The parents and four children repeatedly fled to avoid the fighting, then returned. Finally, they went home to the United States for good in 1940. One year later, Japan bombed the U.S. naval base at Pearl Harbor, bringing the United States into World War II.

When nine-year-old Katherine arrived in Winston-Salem, North Carolina, she wore foreign-looking, secondhand clothes. Her English pronunciation sounded British. Her new classmates heard that she had come from the Far East. That must make her Japanese, they reasoned—the enemy. They tormented her with the nickname "Jap."

She could not change where she had come from. Her parents could not afford to buy her new clothes. She quickly changed the only thing she could: her accent. It was a long time before Katherine made a single friend. This experience of being an outsider is reflected in her novels, most of which are about children as outsiders. "I recognize now that some of my best writing had its seeds in that awful year," she says.[2]

Mr. Womeldorf's work for the Presbyterian Church required the family to move frequently, more than fifteen times during Katherine's childhood. She attended high school in Richmond, Virginia, and Charles Town, West Virginia, then entered King College in Bristol, Tennessee. In college, she acted in plays and sang in choral groups. Challenging teachers encouraged her to analyze and inquire. She

Seventeen-year-old Katherine had already moved more than fifteen times with her family, so she understood how it felt to be the new kid in town. The experience of being an outsider is captured in her novels.

majored in literature and graduated with highest honors in 1954.

Katherine taught sixth grade in rural Virginia for a year. Then she felt ready for her true calling, doing missionary work abroad, as her parents had. She attended graduate school at the Presbyterian School of Christian Education to earn a master's degree. One professor suggested that Katherine make writing her career. Katherine compared herself to the great writers she had studied and asked herself, "How could I dare compete?" She did not want to be mediocre.[3] "But Katherine," the professor prodded, "maybe [writing is] what God is calling you to do." Years later, she realized, "I had to take the risk of being mediocre in order to achieve anything at all."[4]

The Presbyterian Church sent her to Japan in 1957. Before she could go into rural villages, however, she had to study the Japanese language. She studied for two full years. At last, she received her assignment, to the island province of Shikoku. There, she traveled from church to church by motor scooter, preaching and teaching Bible classes. It was much like the work her father had done in China some twenty-five years earlier, only her father had traveled by donkey.

Katherine grew to love the Japanese people and their culture. When she returned to the United States in 1961, she again felt like an outsider. Accustomed to sleeping on a floor mat in Japan, she found a bed uncomfortable. Now her thoughts came first in

Japanese. She struggled to express herself in rusty English. Mission regulations required her to spend a year back in the United States before returning to Japan. She enrolled at Union Theological Seminary in New York City for further study.

One evening, a young clergyman, John Paterson, arrived to play cards with Katherine's roommates. He found himself attracted to Katherine instead and asked her out. After their lunch date the next day, he invited her to visit his church over the Easter holiday. Katherine was a little nervous.[5] She believed Paterson was very serious about her, yet she felt she hardly knew him. Over the Easter visit, she too fell in love. They were married after a three-month courtship, on July 14, 1962.

The Patersons decided at the beginning of their marriage to try to adopt two children and give birth to two. They applied for a baby from a Hong Kong orphanage. While waiting for the baby to arrive, Katherine became pregnant. A son, John Jr., was born in 1964. Six months later, two-year-old Lin from Hong Kong joined the family.

The family moved to Takoma Park, Maryland, where John Paterson became pastor of a Presbyterian church. It was then, with two small children at home, that Katherine Paterson began writing. The same professor who had admired her work recommended her to write books for Sunday school children.

A second son, David, was born in 1966. The Patersons adopted a daughter, Mary, who is of mixed Apache-Kiowa ancestry, in 1968. Katherine Paterson literally snatched writing time in fifteen-minute bits, between diapering and carpooling. Yet she would not have had it any other way. She says that she did not view her obligations as a wife and mother as dreaded chores. Instead, she loved the form they gave to her life.[6]

Paterson soon determined to write what she loved to read—fiction. She wrote and wrote for several years. No publishing houses showed interest in her work. Finally, a friend invited her to join a class for writers of children's books.

For that course, Paterson wrote her first novel for children, *The Sign of the Chrysanthemum*. Each week she wrote one chapter for class. This story of a boy searching for his samurai father was rejected repeatedly by publishers for two years. At last, it was accepted and published in 1973. The next year she wrote *Of Nightingales That Weep*. Both books were historical novels set in Japan.

Her children, then school-age, clamored for her to write a mystery next. While writing the first draft, Paterson was diagnosed with cancer. She was operated on successfully. That summer, on the family vacation, Paterson continued to work on her mystery. One night the power failed. The children became nervous and bored, so Paterson began to read them her story by candlelight. "The next day I found John, who was ten, going through the desk, looking for the manuscript," she said. "He couldn't wait until night to find out what happened next."[7] This book, *The Master Puppeteer,* won the National Book Award when it was published in 1976.

That same year, soon after David Paterson had finished second grade, his best friend, Lisa Hill, was killed by lightning. David's grief and slow healing, as well as Paterson's own brush with death, led to her next novel, *Bridge to Terabithia,* published in 1977.

"I'm not sure I can tell this story. The pain is too fresh," she wrote as she struggled to begin. "But I want to try. For David, for Lisa, for Lisa's mother, and for me."[8] This story of a special friendship won the Newbery Medal.

When the Patersons took in two Cambodian brothers awaiting adoption, it proved a greater challenge than they expected. Every time a new problem arose, Paterson would try to ignore it because the boys were to be in her care only briefly. Later, she felt guilty that she had not made more of an effort to help them. She used her writing to make up for her failure. She decided to create the world's greatest foster mother. This great mother met the world's worst foster child in Paterson's 1978 novel, *The Great Gilly Hopkins,* winner of the National Book Award.

John Paterson went to a new church in 1979. The family moved to Norfolk, Virginia, on the Chesapeake Bay. Katherine Paterson set her next novel, *Jacob Have I Loved,* on an island in the bay.

This story of rival twin sisters, published in 1980, won the 1981 Newbery Medal. Since *The Great Gilly Hopkins* had been a 1979 Newbery Honor Book, this led to her third appearance at the Newbery award ceremony in four years. "We have got to stop meeting like this," she joked to her audience.[9]

The family stayed in Norfolk until John Paterson's final move, in 1985, to a church in Barre, Vermont. During the 1990s, Katherine Paterson set three historical novels in her new home state: *Lyddie, Jip: His Story,* and *Preacher's Boy.* The Patersons remained in Vermont after John Paterson's 1995 retirement.

The Patersons' children grew up, went to college, and three of them married. The Patersons have three grandchildren. David, an actor and playwright, also gave his mother a special gift. He dramatized *The Great Gilly Hopkins* as a musical, and it was a hit in New York City in 1997.

Paterson continues to do the work God called her to do, as her professor suggested forty years before. "I am a Christian," she says, "so that conviction will pervade [my books] even when I make no conscious effort to teach or preach."[10]

Paterson, whose works have been translated into twenty-six languages, received children's literature's highest honor in 1998, when she won the Hans Christian Andersen Medal. The International Board on Books for Young People (IBBY) gives this award

Paterson autographs a copy of *Lyddie*, her novel about a farm girl in the 1840s who takes a job in a factory.

every other year to the author and illustrator who contribute most to literature for the world's children.

Paterson loves to read. She loves to sing and belongs to the church choir. She plays the piano and tennis, both "badly," she says.[11] She enjoys quilting on long winter nights.

More than anything else, she loves to write. "I'm spoiled. I work at home in my own study, wearing whatever I please. I never have to call in sick," she says. "I am the most fortunate person in the world to have been given such work to do."[12]

7

Gary Paulsen

Day 17 of the Iditarod—the annual sled-dog race covering nearly eleven hundred miles from Anchorage to Nome, Alaska. Gary Paulsen's fifteen dogs had survived eighteen-hour days in bitter cold. Paulsen had survived hallucinations and injury from lack of sleep. The final leg of the race followed Alaska's west coast. To the right of the musher and his team towered sheer cliffs. On his left churned the frigid Bering Sea. Under his feet lay the ice-slicked beach. All day, the team ran. As night fell, the lights of Nome, their destination, twinkled in the distance. Paulsen called his team to a halt. They stood waiting. Paulsen did not want the race, grueling as it was, to end. "The journey is everything," he says.[1]

Gary Paulsen

Gary Paulsen's journey began in Minneapolis, Minnesota, on May 17, 1939. His father, Oscar Paulsen, a career Army officer, left to fight in World War II shortly after his son's birth. Gary would not see him again for seven years.

Eunice Paulsen, Gary's mother, was ferociously devoted to her son, who was often sick as a toddler. Later, she would beat to unconsciousness a drunken man who cornered four-year-old Gary in an alley. Yet the war left her so lonely that she parked Gary with a drunken baby-sitter when she went to work in a factory that made ammunition for the military.[2]

World War II ended in 1945, but Oscar Paulsen did not return home. The Army assigned him to the postwar rebuilding of the Philippines. Mrs. Paulsen took Gary there by ship to reunite with her husband.

In the middle of the Pacific, Gary and his mother witnessed a planeload of military wives and children crash-land in the ocean. As lifeboats from the ship sped to the rescue, sharks attacked and mauled the survivors. For eighteen hours, as Gary watched, Mrs. Paulsen helped the medical corpsmen save as many lives as possible. "Your mother was splendid," the captain told Gary.[3] As an adult, Paulsen still suffers nightmares based on this horrible experience.

In the war-ravaged Philippines, Gary was one of a handful of American children. His aloof father worked long hours and drank heavily. So did his mother, who spent her days playing cards with the other officers' wives. Gary was left in the servants' care. After four years, Mrs. Paulsen could stand the bleakness and isolation no longer. She and Gary returned to the United States in 1949. Her husband followed them later and retired from the Army.

Gary, at age ten, had never attended school. Tutors had met with him irregularly in the Philippines. At the various midwestern schools he attended as his father drifted from job to job, Gary was a poor student and unpopular. "I was the geek," he says.[4]

Meanwhile, both his parents had become "puking . . . fighting" drunks.[5] "I never saw my parents sober," Paulsen says.[6] Every summer, to get away from them, Gary found a relative willing to take him in. From these uncles, aunts, and cousins, he developed a love of the family farm, wildlife, and the outdoors.

One winter night, the teenaged Gary entered his town's public library to warm up. The librarian approached him and asked if he would like a library card. When he accepted her offer, she suggested he borrow a western. Gary could barely read, but he took the book home to his basement hideaway. He had fixed up a retreat in his apartment building's basement to get away from his parents. There, he slowly, painstakingly, began to read. It took a month to finish that one book, but Gary was hooked. After that, the librarian supplied Gary with westerns and science fiction and other books. "I can't even describe how liberating it was," he remembers. Like a man dying of thirst, he says, "I drank and drank."[7]

Gary just managed to graduate from high school in Thief River Falls, Minnesota, in 1957. Quickly, he flunked out of nearby Bemidji State Teacher's College. Then he joined the Army and served for four years.

With the aerospace electronics skills he acquired in the military, Paulsen went to work for several high-tech California companies. He married and had two children, a son and a daughter. One night, during a lull as he tracked satellites by computer, Paulsen read a magazine article about flight-testing. He could write something like this, he realized.[8] He quit his job that very night.

Paulsen left for Hollywood. With a made-up résumé, he got a job as a proofreader for a group of men's adventure magazines. Several editors there saw his determination and helped teach him the craft of writing.

His first marriage ended. Paulsen remarried, and he and his new wife withdrew to a cabin in the Minnesota wilderness. He wrote and sold his first book, for adults, on the missile industry in 1967. Then, as he became increasingly successful writing for magazines, the Paulsens moved to Taos, New Mexico.

There, he succumbed to the disease of his parents—alcoholism. His drinking grew so bad that he could not write, so he worked construction. His second marriage ended. He met and wed his third wife, artist Ruth Wright. Their son, Jim, was born in 1971. Still Paulsen drank. Finally, he acknowledged his addiction to alcohol and got help. He dates his sobriety to May 5, 1973.

The drinking years, however, had destroyed Paulsen's ability to write. He had to relearn his skills from the beginning. Slowly, he began to win book and magazine article contracts again. By 1975, he was once more making his living as a professional writer. He published several young adult books in the seventies.

Then disaster struck again. Paulsen signed a long-term contract with a publisher who did not pay him as promised. Then he was sued for libel by a man who claimed he had been fictionalized as a Paulsen book character. Though the suit was dismissed, Paulsen became disgusted with the publishing industry. Deeply in debt, he fled again, with his family, to the Minnesota woods. Desperately poor, the Paulsens lived off the land, without plumbing or electricity.

To earn a few dollars, Paulsen began trapping predatory animals for the state. At first, he worked his trapline on foot. Then a friend gave him a broken sled and four dogs. Paulsen fell in love with mushing, which he calls the "ancient and beautiful" experience of running sled dogs.[9]

Soon he was spending days away from home, in awe of the grandeur and mystery of the woods. "It was as if everything that had happened to me before ceased to exist," he says.[10] Finally, he could no longer bring himself to kill animals. He gave up trapping and instead ran his dogs for sheer pleasure and in local races. Then he heard about the Iditarod.

Paulsen began to train for this most-challenging of races. To enter would require $14,000 for equipment and expenses. After he published an article called "The Deer," Paulsen unexpectedly received a call from an editor who had read it. Richard Jackson asked if he was doing any writing for young people. No, Paulsen answered, and explained that he was raising money and training for the Iditarod. Jackson sent Paulsen the full amount he required. Give me the first look at your next book, Jackson wrote.[11]

Paulsen turned back to writing, this time by firelight as he huddled with his dogs in the freezing cold. Book after book poured from him. *Dancing Carl* and *Buttermilk Days and Popcorn Nights* appeared in 1983, the year he ran his first Iditarod. *Tracker* was published in 1984, when he was in training for his second Iditarod, which he ran the next year.

Dogsong (1985) won Paulsen the first of his three Newbery Honor awards. The germ of this book grew from an experience during his first Iditarod. Near the end of the race, an Inuit (Eskimo) boy asked Paulsen to teach him about dogs. Paulsen said he was appalled that a native Alaskan would have to get this knowledge from "some white jerk from Minnesota."[12] *Dogsong*, the story of an Inuit youth

Editor Richard Jackson, left, sent Paulsen enough money to enter the 1983 Iditarod sled-dog race. In return, said Jackson, "when you get around to writing something, let me be the first to see it."

who embraces mushing as a return to traditional ways, sold well enough to put the Paulsens back on firm financial footing.

Paulsen's second Newbery Honor came for *Hatchet*, published in 1987. Equally popular with critics and readers, it has become one of the best-selling young adult novels of all time. In it, thirteen-year-old Brian Robeson's plane crashes in the Canadian wilderness. The only other passenger, the pilot, is killed. Brian survives alone, armed only with his hatchet, until his rescue. Paulsen takes pride in having tested every one of Brian's experiences himself, including eating raw turtle eggs. "Pretty rank," he admits.[13]

Readers have clamored for sequels and have gotten them. *The River* and *Brian's Return* describe Brian's life after his rescue. *Brian's Winter* takes the unusual tactic of reworking *Hatchet* as if Brian had not been rescued before cold weather set in. Instead, it explores what it might have been like for Brian to survive alone all winter.

In 1990, Paulsen was diagnosed with heart disease. Doctors forced him to give up running sled dogs. The Iditarod had changed him, however. He had trained himself to need only four hours of sleep. He was now "absolutely driven," he says.[14] The energy he once expended on mushing is now fully channeled into writing.

To tear himself away from the page, Paulsen throws himself into projects. He builds sailboats and

Paulsen wears one of his favorite caps—"Read Like a Wolf Eats"—
as he signs books for his fans in 1997.

antique-style cars. He takes long-distance motorcycle trips and sails the Pacific. Then, of course, he writes about his experiences. To date, this dedication has resulted in more than 180 books.

The American Library Association honored Paulsen with the Margaret A. Edwards Award in 1997. This recognizes his lifetime achievement as a writer for young adults. The books the committee chose as his finest were *Dancing Carl, Hatchet, The Crossing, The Winter Room* (his third Newbery Honor Book), *Woodsong,* and *Canyons.*

The Paulsens moved back to New Mexico in 1991. They divide their time between a ranch in the mountains and a catamaran in the Pacific. The boat is one of Paulsen's favorite places to write. "I [even] wrote in a full-force-eight storm," he says. "I love it. The hair goes up on the back of my neck when I work, even after [all these years]."[15]

Gary Soto

┌─────────┐
│ **8** │
└─────────┘

Gary Soto

G ary Soto's father, Manuel, had worked hard all afternoon, planting a lawn for his new house. He showed his five-year-old son how to hook his thumb over the hose's nozzle to water it with a fine spray. Gary watched his father sit down, resting with an iced tea. "His knees were water-stained and his chest was flecked with mud," he remembered. "Mom sat next to him. . . . He patted his lap, and she jumped into it girlishly, arms around his neck."[1] The next day an industrial accident severely injured Manuel Soto. He lingered for two days, then died.

Gary Soto was born in Fresno, California, on April 12, 1952. Although his grandparents had been born in Mexico, both his parents were California natives. His father's death plunged the family into poverty. His mother, Angie, was forced to work long hours in the fields and food processing plants to support her children. Gary had an older brother, Rick, and a younger sister, Debra. The children often had to stay home alone. They did not want to get their mother in trouble with the authorities, so they told no one that they could not afford day care.

Gary's parents had spoken primarily English at home. He picked up Spanish from the many relatives living nearby. "We were pretty much an illiterate family," he says. "We didn't have books, and no one encouraged us to read."[2]

When Gary was in grade school his mother married again. Her new husband was an Anglo. The family moved from the barrio, or Spanish-speaking section, to an ethnically mixed Fresno neighborhood. Gary's half brother, Jimmy, was born soon after.

The Soto children spent hours roaming the city streets in search of adventure. Summers they passed with games and crafts at the local playground. Gary and Rick tried out year after year for an elite baseball team. "Year after year we failed to impress the coaches," he lamented.[3] The brothers joined an all-Chicano team instead. As its season progressed, though, too many losses caused their teammates to slink away. Soon the Sotos were the only players left.

Gary attended first Catholic school, then public school. He was not a good student. Neither his family nor the school system expected much of him.

Their hope was that "if we stayed out of prison, we would be fine," he says. Then "there was a reason to be proud [of us]."[4]

At Roosevelt High School, Gary joined the wrestling team. He hung out with his friends, attended school dances, and admired pretty girls, mostly from afar. He had no particular plans for his future. During high school, he began to spend summers working in the fields to buy new clothes for school. Hoeing and harvesting under the broiling sun was backbreaking work. To motivate himself, Gary imagined his "wardrobe . . . crisp and bright in the closet," he remembers.[5]

As a teenager, Gary fought with his stepfather. After his junior year, the conflict became too great. Gary ran away. He landed near Los Angeles in Glendale, California, where he found a job at a tire factory. The workers there breathed in toxic fumes all day and became coated in black, powdery filth. "There was something worse than field work," Gary realized.[6] He went home to Fresno to finish high school.

What would his future be? Would he "marry Mexican poor, work Mexican hours, and in the end die a Mexican death, broke and in despair?" he wondered.[7] In 1970, young men who were not students were being drafted into the military by the U.S. government, which required them to become involved in the war effort. Gary enrolled in Fresno City

College in order to escape fighting in the Vietnam War. He worked part-time and lived at home.

One day, he was browsing in the college library. A book of modern poems by American authors caught his eye. The poems resembled nothing he had ever read. They were "rambunctious, lively, irreverent," he remembers.[8] As he read, he saw his own feelings of strangeness and confusion reflected in the poems. He realized he was not the only one who felt that way. It was "a human pain," he realized.[9] Excitement gripped him. "Wow, wow, wow. I [want] to do this thing," he thought.[10]

Soto began writing and studying literature in junior college. Then he transferred to California State University, at Fresno. One of his professors, Philip Levine, a noted poet himself, encouraged the young writer. Soto graduated with honors in 1974.

Soto married his college sweetheart, Carolyn Oda, in 1975. A Japanese-American, Oda trained as an artist and editor. The following year, Soto received his master's degree in fine arts (creative writing) from the University of California at Irvine. "I was living for poetry—determined to go all the way," he says.[11]

He got his big break when his first book of poetry, *The Elements of San Joaquin*, was published in 1977. Reviewers praised the excellence and uniqueness of his poetry, which was based on the lives of Chicano farmworkers and barrio dwellers. The collection won several awards.

It seemed "my days in the grape and cotton fields were a thing of the past," Soto remembers. The local newspaper published an article about Soto's success. "[My] friends were amazed that I had made the inside of the newspaper without being [in] trouble!"[12] When Soto presented a copy of his first book to his grandmother, she proudly placed it in a picture frame on her coffee table, but was unable to read it. Since fleeing the Mexican Revolution as a teenager, she had never learned to read in Spanish or English.

In 1977, Soto began teaching at the University of California at Berkeley. He and his wife had a daughter, Mariko. Soto won a prestigious literary award, the Guggenheim, in 1979, which allowed the family to live in Mexico City for six months.

After he published four more poetry collections, Soto decided to "do something different."[13] He wrote a collection of short prose pieces about his life, mainly his Fresno childhood and youth. Published by a small press in 1985, *Living Up the Street* became "an underground classic," Soto says.[14] The steady stream of letters he received from Chicano teens who loved the book convinced him to try writing for young people.

Baseball in April and Other Stories, his first book for teens, was published in 1990. Set in the Fresno barrio, each story focuses on a happiness or heartache of growing up. The title story strongly resembles the baseball adventures of the Soto brothers many years before. The collection won the Beatty Award, which honors the year's best book with a California setting. "I began to feel like I was doing something valuable," Soto says.[15]

Soto quit his professorship to write and visit schools full-time in 1991. He estimates that since his first book for young people was published, he has spoken to more than three hundred thousand students and teachers. At the Fresno elementary school that Soto had attended, the vice principal surprised him by introducing his high school wrestling coach. "Oh, Gary was a good wrestler," the coach assured the audience. "What's a little lie between old friends?" Soto added.[16]

He followed the success of *Baseball in April* with *Taking Sides* in 1991. In it, athlete Lincoln Mendoza must deal with conflicting loyalties when the basketball team at his new, suburban school plays the team from his old, barrio school. Lincoln reappeared in 1992's *Pacific Crossing* to study karate and travel to Japan. Soto himself is a student of the martial arts with a black belt in tae kwan do.

Soto has published three books of poetry for young people: 1991's *A Fire in My Hands*, 1992's *Neighborhood Odes*, and 1995's *Canto Familiar*. He has written two novels about troubled teens, *Jesse* in 1995 and *Buried Onions* in 1997. In the 1990s, Soto also published picture books and made three short films based on his writings. One of these, *The Pool Party*, won the Carnegie Medal for best children's short film of the year.

Soto's poems and stories capture Mexican-American life and culture.

Soto lives in Berkeley with his family. He writes in the morning, tackles correspondence in the afternoon, and spends most evenings with his wife and daughter. He teaches English to Latino children and adults at his church.

Soto has not abandoned writing poetry for adults. In 1995, his collection *New and Selected Poems* was a finalist for the National Book Award, one of adult literature's highest honors. Just as he was once on fire for poetry, he is now also on fire for young people's literature.

"My business is to make readers out of non-readers," he says. "To start Chicanos reading." He imagines what might happen if this transformation occurred as it did in his own life. He imagines "a family whose grandmother, an illiterate, fits a book into a picture frame, the centerpiece for a household that will in time . . . throw open the cover."[17]

9

R. L. Stine

Three-year-old Bob Stine settled down for his afternoon nap. His mother read him a chapter of his favorite book, *Pinocchio*, as she did every day. Little Bob hung on every word as the wooden puppet in the story sat down and put his feet up on the stove. When the puppet fell asleep, his wooden feet burned off! Mrs. Stine was not reading from the sweetened Walt Disney movie version of the story. She was reading the original tale by Carlo Collodi. It was "gruesome," R. L. Stine remembers.[1] "Very influential in my writing."[2]

Robert Laurence Stine was born on October 8, 1943, in Columbus, Ohio. His father, Lewis, worked for a restaurant supply company, and his mother,

R. L. Stine

Anne, was a homemaker. Eventually, Bob had a brother, Bill, three years younger, and a sister, Pam, seven years younger. The Stines lived in Bexley, Ohio, a wealthy suburb of Columbus. Though their house was smaller than their neighbors' houses and their lifestyle more modest, Lewis and Anne Stine provided a happy, comfortable life for their children.

Bob had normal childhood fears—big dogs, swimming lessons, the dark, forbidden attic. "Nothing too scary," he says.[3] But from an early age, he loved to give himself goose bumps. The Stines did not buy a television set until Bob was nine. Before that, he spent hours listening to plays on the radio.

Every week, he tuned in to a radio show called *Suspense*. It began with the sound of a gong, then a deep, chilling voice slowly announced, "And now . . . tales . . . calculated . . . to keep you . . . in *suspense!*" Bob was so terrified by the show's introduction that he flicked the radio off and never listened to a single episode. "Today, I try to make my books as scary as that announcer's voice," he says.[4]

When Bob was in grade school, he found an old typewriter. With one finger, he began to pound out stories, comics, and magazines. Bob's first magazine was called *The All New Bob Stine Giggle Book*. He still owns the only copy, which measures three inches by four inches.

Bob's writing models were *Mad* magazine and the gory EC horror comics, including *Tales from the Crypt*. His mother forbade him to bring these home, declaring them "trash." Luckily, Bob discovered that they were available at the barbershop. Every week, he read his favorite magazines from cover to cover before getting a quick trim. "As a result, I had even less hair than I do now," he says.[5]

Even when he was a kid, writing was Bob's passion. He scored B's on his report card without much study. His main interest in school was getting laughs by making jokes and passing around his homemade humor comics. What did his parents make of this? "They kept telling me to go out and play!" he says.[6] But secretly they were proud. At thirteen, Bob had his bar mitzvah service, becoming an adult in the Jewish faith. As a gift, his parents gave him a heavy-duty, office-quality typewriter, just what he wanted. In high school, he told them he could not get a summer job because he was writing a novel. The Stines accepted this explanation without question.

Bob graduated from high school in Bexley in 1961. For college, he chose Ohio State University in nearby Columbus. Not only could he live at home, he could write for Ohio State's famous humor magazine, *Sundial*. After a year of writing for the magazine, sometimes producing entire issues by himself, Stine became editor in chief. He held the post for three years.

After graduating from Ohio State in 1965, Stine wanted to move to New York City. "I figured that's where writers lived," he said.[7] To save money for the move, Stine became a high school substitute teacher.

He used the experience to eavesdrop on students' conversations. He credits this year with giving him a good ear for how kids really talk. He also enjoyed swapping comic books with his students.

Stine's goal when he moved to New York in 1966 was to edit his own humor magazine. To gain experience, he first worked for some other magazines, relating investment advice, inventing celebrity interviews, and reporting on soft-drink industry news. Finally, in 1968, he went to work at Scholastic Press magazines, where he would stay for sixteen years.

Meanwhile, at a party on a rainy night, Stine met a beautiful redhead with a terrible cold, Jane Waldhorn. Despite her sniffles, they fell in love. They were married on June 22, 1969.

Stine began his career at Scholastic writing and editing social studies articles. He thrived on the fast pace of weekly magazines. Magazine work does not allow for writer's block, he says, and attributes his ability to write fast to his Scholastic years.[8] Jane Stine also became a Scholastic magazine editor.

After several years, Bob Stine founded and edited a teen humor magazine for Scholastic called *Bananas*. It featured movie parodies, advice given by a dog, and a character named Phil Fly, who begged in every issue not to be swatted. Later, Stine edited a similar magazine called *Maniac*. Though his lifelong dream of editing a humor magazine was fulfilled, Stine had not reached the peak of his career.

Stine started writing when he was young—and he has not stopped.

While working at *Bananas,* Stine received a call from a children's book editor at E. P. Dutton. She asked if he might like to write a humorous children's book for her. Stine decided to write a book he would have found useful as a kid. He filled *How to Be Funny* with tips and quizzes for budding jokesters.

The Stines' only child, Matthew, was born in 1980. When Matthew was little, Stine spent a great deal of time exploring New York with his son. After Scholastic's humor magazines went out of business, Stine worked at home writing children's books. "I don't want a job [when I grow up]," said Matthew. "I want to hang around the house like Dad."[9]

In 1982, Stine became head writer for the children's television show *Eureeka's Castle.* He and his team wrote humorous sketches for the show's cast of puppets. Stine based one of the puppet characters, Batly, on his son. Whenever Batly fell down or ran into something, which was often, he, like Matthew, would jump up and shout, "I meant to do that!"[10] After Stine's staff produced one hundred hours of programming, however, they lost their jobs. No new shows would be made. The original shows would simply be rerun.

Stine resumed writing at home. He produced dozens of joke books, adventure novels in which readers can choose different plotlines, and series books based on television shows, movies, and even toys.

One day, Stine had lunch with a friend who was an editor at Scholastic Books. Horror novels for teenagers were growing in popularity, she said. Why didn't he try his hand at one? She even gave him a title—*Blind Date*. Stine went home and started plotting. *Blind Date* took a month to outline and three months to write, which was slow for Stine. "I didn't really know what I was doing," Stine admits.[11] When it was published in 1986, this story of a boy harassed by phone calls from a dead girl claiming to be his blind date was a smash hit.

Stine followed it up with three more horror novels: *Twisted,* in 1987; *Broken Date,* in 1988; and *The Babysitter,* in 1989. Then his wife asked him to write a horror series for her new publishing company. Jane Stine had quit her editorial job to start Parachute Press. Bob Stine came up with a series title, *Fear Street.* "Where your worst nightmares live," Jane promptly answered when he proposed it to her.[12]

The *Fear Street* books began appearing in 1989. There are more than one hundred titles in print. Stine still writes them at the rate of one a month, and they are one of the most popular teen paperback series in America.

So many younger kids wanted to read *Fear Street* that Stine began a new series for them in 1992—*Goosebumps.* The books were an immediate sensation. Even with their cliffhanger chapter endings and roller-coaster-like suspense, Stine believes the stories are "safe scares."[13] He adds, "I'm very careful never to make these books too REAL. . . . [I] keep many real-world problems, such as drug abuse or alcoholism, out."[14]

Stine also writes one *Goosebumps* book a month. Luckily, he never lacks for ideas. Sometimes just a single image gives him his idea. The mental picture of a bathtub full of worms suggested *Go Eat Worms.* Sometimes real events are the trigger. One Halloween, Matthew Stine wore a green rubber Frankenstein mask. When he could not take it off, Stine had his inspiration for *The Haunted Mask.*

Goosebumps is the top-selling young people's book series in history, with more than two hundred million copies in print. Stine followed it with the *Goosebumps 2000* series in 1998. It has inspired a television series, toys, and a ride at Disney-MGM Studios. The books have even been packed into bags of Doritos tortilla chips.

Stine receives more than one thousand fan letters a week. Many of them are from parents thanking him for turning their kids into readers. These kids, particularly boys, never read anything before they encountered R. L. Stine. "I'm very proud of the fact that I created something to help get boys reading," he says.[15] One boy who *never* reads R. L. Stine is his son, Matthew. "He knows it drives me CRAZY!" says his dad.[16]

Though he has no plans to retire, Stine knows that the *Goosebumps* phenomenon cannot last forever. In fact, "I'm sort of counting on it [ending]," he says. "Then I can take it easy."[17]

Laurence Yep

10

Laurence Yep

Little Laurence Yep sat in front of the television set watching a cartoon show that featured a character named Scrappy. Laurence laughed as Scrappy battled a pack of Chinese laundrymen. The funny-looking laundrymen, with their black pajamas and eyes drawn like slits, amused him. He pulled up the corners of his own eyes and made a face. "You're Chinese," Laurence Yep's mother exclaimed in shock. "Stop that."[1] Laurence was too young to realize that the cartoon showed an insulting stereotype of his own ethnic group.

The Yeps spoke English at home. At that time, they were the only Chinese family in their San Francisco neighborhood. Although he saw his

Chinese relatives regularly, Chinese culture did not yet play a role in Laurence's life. "In a sense I have no one culture to call my own since I exist [partly] in several," Yep says. "In my writing I can create my own."[2]

Laurence Yep's mother, Franche Lee, grew up in West Virginia. Her parents had emigrated from China to the United States shortly after the turn of the nineteenth century. Laurence's father, Yep Gim Lew, left China at age ten. Gim Lew changed his name to Thomas Yep upon becoming an American citizen. He met Franche Lee in high school in San Francisco.

Laurence was born in San Francisco on June 14, 1948. The Yeps already had a nine-year-old son, Thomas. They had hoped that Thomas would welcome the new baby if he was permitted to choose its name. Thomas named his brother after a saint he had studied at Catholic school, a martyr who had been grilled alive on a spit. Fortunately, Laurence did not realize this for many years.

Laurence's parents operated a small grocery store in a San Francisco neighborhood called the Western Addition. Originally, this had been a working-class area with blacks, whites, Hispanics, and Asians living side by side. When Laurence was seven, however, almost the whole neighborhood was razed to construct a low-income housing project. Swiftly the area became much poorer. The Yeps stayed, however, and got along well with their new neighbors.

Laurence traveled by bus to a Catholic school in Chinatown. Even there, with an all-Chinese student body, he felt like an outsider. His classmates spoke English but switched to Chinese to imitate the nuns or tell dirty jokes. Still, Laurence stubbornly resisted learning Chinese in class.

One of the places where he found refuge was the Chinatown branch of the public library. He devoured its science fiction collection. "Science fiction was about adapting," he says. "That's what I was doing every time I got off the bus traveling between my two worlds."[3] Family and adventure stories about "typical" American kids seemed ridiculous to him. All their characters roamed freely on bikes and left their front doors unlocked. No one Laurence knew was this foolish! "It was no wonder that I fell in love with stories that involved unicorns and Martians. I was as strange as they were," he says.[4]

As a top student, Laurence was accepted at Saint Ignatius High School. It was run by the Jesuit religious order, and the school was noted for its demanding curriculum and high academic standards. Laurence excelled there in science and writing. During his senior year, his English teacher told the best students, including Laurence, that to earn an A they would have to have a piece of writing accepted for publication by a national magazine. Luckily, the teacher later changed his mind. Laurence's stories had all been rejected.

Still, Laurence so enjoyed writing them that he kept on sending stories out in hopes of publication. "I got bitten by the bug," he says.[5] Laurence found that as he puzzled out a story, he took elements from all the different cultures that influenced him and put them together into a beautiful whole. "When I wrote, I went from being a puzzle to a puzzle solver."[6]

In 1966, he won a college scholarship to another Jesuit school, Marquette University in Milwaukee, Wisconsin. He planned to study journalism and become a professional writer. Wisconsin's frigid winter and Marquette's bleak campus came as a "culture shock," though.[7] So did the nearly all-white student body.

Again, writing provided comfort to Laurence. Longing for his hometown, he wrote a science fiction story about half-dolphin half-humans who survive after an earthquake submerges San Francisco. To his surprise, his story, "The Selkey Kids," was accepted for magazine publication. His pay: a penny a word. He also contributed to the college literary magazine. Its editor, Joanne Ryder, became his close friend, spending hours listening to his problems.

Unable to bear four years at Marquette, Yep transferred to the University of California at Santa Cruz. He received his bachelor's degree there in 1970. Thinking that he would like to become a college professor of English, Yep enrolled in the Ph.D.

program at the State University of New York at Buffalo.

He continued to publish short science fiction in magazines and story collections. Meanwhile, Joanne Ryder had become a children's book editor in New York City. She showed his stories to her boss, who asked Yep to consider writing a science fiction novel for young people. Yep published this first novel, *Sweetwater*, in 1973. This story of a minority race of aliens living temporarily on a distant planet won praise from book reviewers.

In 1975, Yep received his Ph.D. in English and began teaching part-time at two California colleges. The same year, he published his next young adult novel, *Dragonwings*. In writing *Sweetwater*, Yep realized, he had actually cast the story of Chinese-Americans in the West as science fiction. Now he felt ready to "take a razor blade and cut through my defenses" by writing directly about them, and himself.[8]

Dragonwings is based on the story of Fung Joe Guey. This real Chinese immigrant to California built and flew an airplane only a few years after the Wright brothers did. In Yep's historical novel, named a Newbery Honor Book, "Windrider" and his newly arrived ten-year-old son soar out of the situation a racist society puts them in. They "reaffirm the power of the imagination," says Yep.[9]

Yep based the characters of both the father and son on his own father, who also came from China as a child. Thomas Yep excelled in making and flying traditional Chinese kites. He was "master of the winds," says his son.[10]

In *Child of the Owl*, published in 1977, Yep returned to the San Francisco of his 1950s and 1960s childhood. He tells the story of Casey Young, abandoned by her compulsive-gambler father, who moves in with her traditional Chinese grandmother.

Yep modeled the grandmother, Paw-Paw, on his own grandmother, Marie Lee. As a teenage bride, Mrs. Lee had run Chinese laundries with her husband in small American towns. A mixture of the traditional and modern, she taught her grandson the correct Chinese way to cook rice, yet she became a Beatles fan before he did.

Yep considers 1979's *Sea Glass* to be his favorite and most autobiographical novel. He admits that the story of Craig Chin, who moves from San Francisco to a rural town and makes a place for himself between Chinese and white society, hits very "close to home."[11]

During the 1980s, Yep wrote in a variety of genres for young people. He published humor, mystery, fantasy, folklore, even picture books. He also wrote plays, which produced by small California theaters. His greatest success as a playwright came when his adaptation of *Dragonwings* was staged at New York's Lincoln Center. Yep also lectured in Asian-American studies at the University of California at Berkeley.

Yep has written humor, mystery, fantasy, folklore, and even picture books and plays.

Yep's autobiography, *The Lost Garden*, was published in 1991. In 1994, *Dragon's Gate*, a fantasy novel drawing on Chinese mythology, won him his second Newbery Honor award. Still a science fiction buff, he also wrote an adult novel, *Shadow Lord*, based on the television show *Star Trek*.

Yep is the most prominent Asian-American writer for young people. Maxine Hong Kingston, a prizewinning adult-book author, has written that Yep's books have scenes "that will make every Chinese-American child gasp with recognition."[12] Yet Yep intends his books for all teens, since so many young people of all races feel like outsiders. "Many teenagers feel they're aliens," he says.[13]

After many years of friendship, Yep and Joanne Ryder realized they had fallen in love. They married in 1989. Yep says that he and his wife are very different, "yet it would be difficult to think of life without her."[14] Yep and Ryder live in San Francisco, and both are full-time writers. Yep loves music, from classical to rock, and always listens while writing. He enjoys movies and collects toy soldiers.

Ryder loves nature and the outdoors. As a science writer for children, she often does research by volunteering at the San Francisco Zoo. Sometimes she brings her research home. Once, she kept a lizard to study and placed its food—meal worms—in the refrigerator. "I labeled the dish 'LIZARD FOOD. DO NOT OPEN!'" she says, "so my husband who hates being surprised by small creeping creatures would not open it by mistake."[15]

Yep spends so many hours a day writing that he and his wife have to schedule which of the day's three meals they will eat together. He credits his work ethic to the long hours he and his parents put into running their grocery store. "You can't call in sick and you stay at the store twelve and fourteen hours a day. Combine that with my Jesuit education and you have a man who never lets up."[16]

Chapter Notes

Preface

1. *Contemporary Authors* (Detroit: Gale, 1989), vol. 125, p. 425.

2. Stephanie Zvirin, "The *Booklist* Interview: Gary Paulsen," *Booklist,* January 1 and 15, 1999, p. 864.

Chapter 1. Judy Blume

1. Maryann N. Weidt, *Presenting Judy Blume* (Boston: Twayne, 1990), p. 52.

2. Ibid., p. 57.

3. Ibid., p. 12.

4. Judy Blume, *Letters to Judy* (New York: Pocket Books, 1986), p. 15.

5. "Starring Judy Blume As Herself," *Gurl Magazine,* <http://www.gurl.com/magzine/where/features/blume/books.html> (March 9, 1999).

6. Blume, *Letters to Judy,* p. 134.

7. Ibid.

8. "Judy Blume Forever," <http://www.bostonwomen.com/blume.html> (March 9, 1999).

9. Betsy Lee, *Judy Blume's Story* (Minneapolis: Dillon, 1981), p. 94.

10. Ellen Barry, "Judy Blume for President," *Boston Phoenix,* May 21–28, 1998, <www.bostonphoenix.com/archive/features/98/05/21/JUDY_BLUME.html> (March 8, 1999).

11. Adi Bloom, "Superfudge and Apple Pie," *Hilary,* Issue 1, 1997, <http://www.cherwell.ospl.co.uk/archive/Hilary1997/Issue1/comment/article2.html> (March 8, 1999).

12. Weidt, p. 91.

13. "Starring Judy Blume As Herself."

14. Blume, *Letters to Judy*, p. 125.
15. Ibid., p. 126.
16. "Starring Judy Blume As Herself."
17. Ibid.
18. Roger Sutton, "Forever Yours: An Interview with Judy Blume," *School Library Journal*, June 1996, p. 26.
19. Barry, "Judy Blume for President."

Chapter 2. Virginia Hamilton

1. Rudine S. Bishop, "Virginia Hamilton," *The Horn Book*, July/August 1995, p. 443.
2. Ibid.
3. "A Conversation with Virginia Hamilton" (New York: Scholastic Press, 1998), p. 3.
4. Tracy Hoffman, "An Exclusive Interview With Virginia Hamilton," <http://<www.wordmuseum.com/virginiahamiltoninterview.htm> (March 23, 1999).
5. Virginia Hamilton, "Welcome to My World," <http://www.virginiahamilton.com> (January 9, 1999).
6. "Contemporary Authors Interview," *Contemporary Authors* (Detroit: Gale, 1987), vol. 20, p. 209.
7. Nina Mikkelsen, *Virginia Hamilton* (New York: Twayne, 1994), p. 10.
8. Nina Mikkelsen, "A Conversation With Virginia Hamilton," *Youth Services in Libraries*, Summer 1994, p. 400.
9. Paul Heins, "Virginia Hamilton," *The Horn Book*, August 1975, p. 346.
10. Ibid.
11. "Contemporary Authors Interview," p. 210.
12. Virginia Hamilton, "Laura Ingalls Wilder Medal Acceptance Speech," *The Horn Book*, July/August 1995, p. 436.
13. Mikkelsen, *Virginia Hamilton*, p. 8.
14. "A Visit With Virginia Hamilton," <http://www.virginiahamilton.com/pages/biostuff.htm> (January 9, 1999).

15. "Contemporary Authors Interview," p. 211.
16. "Leigh and Jaime Levi," <http://www.virginia hamilton.com/pages/kids.htm> (January 9, 1999).
17. Hoffman.

Chapter 3. Julius Lester

1. Julius Lester, *Lovesong* (New York: Arcade, 1988), p. 9.
2. Ibid., pp. 10–11.
3. Ibid., p. 12.
4. Julius Lester, *All Is Well* (New York: Morrow, 1976), p. 13.
5. Ibid.
6. Ibid., p. 18.
7. Ibid., p. 11.
8. Julius Lester, *Falling Pieces of the Broken Sky* (New York: Arcade, 1990), p. 70.
9. Barry List, "Julius Lester," *Publishers Weekly,* February 12, 1988, p. 67.
10. Lester, *Falling Pieces of the Broken Sky,* p. 79.
11. Julius Lester, *To Be a Slave* (Thirtieth Anniversary Edition) (New York: Dial, 1998), p. 7.
12. "Julius Lester: Newbery Runner-up," *School Library Journal,* May 1969, p. 57.
13. Lester, *To Be a Slave,* p. 13.
14. List, p. 68.
15. *The Fourth Book of Junior Authors and Illustrators* (New York: Wilson, 1978), p. 223.
16. Lester, *Lovesong,* p. 160.
17. Ibid., p. 225.
18. Michael Cart, "To Be a Slave," *Booklist,* February 15, 1999, p. 1052.

Chapter 4. Lois Lowry

1. *A Visit with Lois Lowry* (videocassette) (Boston: Houghton Mifflin, 1985).

2. Internet Public Library Youth Division: Ask the Author, "Lois Lowry," <http://www.ipl.org/youth/AskAuthor/Lowry.html> (January 22, 2000).

3. Lois Lowry, *Looking Back* (Boston: Houghton Mifflin, 1998), p. 114.

4. *Something About the Author: Autobiography Series* (Detroit: Gale, 1987), vol. 3, p. 140.

5. Ibid., p. 141.

6. Lois Lowry, "How Does It Feel to Be on a TV Quiz Show? Don't Ask," *The New York Times*, March 31, 1974, p. 23.

7. Joel D. Chaston, *Lois Lowry* (New York: Twayne, 1997), p. 12.

8. *Something About the Author*, p. 142.

9. *A Visit with Lois Lowry*.

10. Lowry, p. 142.

11. Lois Lowry, "Newbery Medal Acceptance," *The Horn Book*, July/August 1994, pp. 414–416.

12. Chaston, p. 20.

13. Lowry, Lois, "A Message from the Author," <http://www.bdd.com/bin/forums/teachers/give.html> (August 25, 1998).

14. Lowry, *Looking Back*, p. 168.

15. Ibid., p. 181.

Chapter 5. Phyllis Reynolds Naylor

1. Phyllis Reynolds Naylor, *How I Came to Be a Writer* (New York: Atheneum, 1978), p. 6–7.

2. Ibid., p. 12.

3. Ibid., p. 26.

4. Ibid., p. 27.

5. *Something About the Author: Autobiography Series,* (Detroit: Gale, 1990), vol. 10, p. 193.

6. Naylor, p. 60.

7. Ibid., p. 61.

8. Rex Naylor, "Phyllis Reynolds Naylor," *The Horn Book*, July/August 1992, p. 413.

9. "Phyllis Reynolds Naylor," <http://www.bdd.com/bin/forums/teachers/nayl.html> (November 18, 1998).

10. "Phyllis Reynolds Naylor," <http://www.childrensbookguild.org/PhyllisNaylor.html> (November 18, 1998).

11. *Something About the Author*, p. 191.

12. "Phyllis Reynolds Naylor," <http://www.childrensbookguild.org>.

13. Phyllis Reynolds Naylor, "Newbery Acceptance Speech," *The Horn Book*, July/August 1992, p. 407.

14. Ibid., p. 406.

15. Ibid., p. 405.

16. Internet Public Library Youth Division: Ask the Author, "Phyllis Reynolds Naylor," <http://www.ipl.org/youth/AskAuthor/Naylor.html> (November 18, 1998).

17. *Naylor, How I Came to Be a Writer*, p. 132.

Chapter 6. Katherine Paterson

1. Katherine Paterson, *A Sense of Wonder* (New York: Plume, 1995), p. 145.

2. Ibid., p. 142.

3. Ibid., p. viii.

4. Brigette Weeks, "Making of a Master," *Washington Post*, May 14, 1977, p. B3.

5. Alice Cary, *Katherine Paterson* (Santa Barbara: Learning Works, 1997), p. 93.

6. Paterson, p. 42.

7. Ibid., p. 98.

8. Ibid., p. 105.

9. Ibid., p. 126.

10. "Questions and Answers," <http://www.terabithia.com/questions.htm> (September 22, 1998).

11. "Questions and Answers," <http://www.terabithia.com/questions.htm> (August 25, 1998).

12. Internet Public Library Youth Division: Ask the Author, "Katherine Paterson," <http://www.ipl.org/youth/AskAuthor/paterson.html> (August 25, 1998).

Chapter 7. Gary Paulsen

1. Gary Salvner, *Presenting Gary Paulsen* (New York: Twayne, 1996), p. 38.

2. Gary Paulsen, *Eastern Sun, Winter Moon* (New York: Harcourt Brace Jovanovich, 1993), p. 1.

3. Ibid., p. 61.

4. David Gale, "The Maximum Expression of Being Human," *School Library Journal*, June 1997, p. 26.

5. Rebecca Bain, "Paulsen Pauses to Smile," *Children's Librarian*, May/June 1998, p. 1.

6. Martin Arnold, "Finding Stories Boys Will Read," *The New York Times*, October 15, 1998, p. E3.

7. *Something About the Author* (Detroit: Gale, 1995), vol. 79, p. 162.

8. Salvner, p. 17.

9. Ibid., p. 24.

10. *Something About the Author*, p. 163.

11. Salvner, p. 26.

12. Ibid., p. 73.

13. Ibid., p. 44.

14. Stephanie Zvirin, "The Booklist Interview: Gary Paulsen," *Booklist*, January 1 and 15, 1999, p. 864.

15. Ibid.

Chapter 8. Gary Soto

1. Gary Soto, *Living Up the Street* (New York: Dell, 1985), p. 38.

2. *Contemporary Authors* (Detroit: Gale, 1989), vol. 125, p. 425.

3. Soto, p. 46.

4. Don Lee, "About Gary Soto," *Ploughshares*, Spring 1995, p. 188.

5. Soto, p. 103.

6. Ibid., p. 123.

7. Ibid., pp. 119–120.

8. *Contemporary Authors,* p. 425.

9. *Dictionary of Literary Biography* (Detroit: Gale, 1989), vol. 82, p. 247.

10. Lee, p. 189.

11. "BantamDoubledayDell Presents Gary Soto" (New York: BantamDoubledayDell, 1994), p. 2.

12. The Official Gary Soto Website <www.garysoto.com/whatsup.html> (December 15, 1998).

13. Soto, pp. 161–163.

14. *Contemporary Authors,* p. 426.

15. The Official Gary Soto Website (December 15, 1998).

16. Lee, p. 189.

17. The Official Gary Soto Website (January 9, 1999).

18. Ibid.

Chapter 9. R. L. Stine

1. "R. L. Stine," <http://www.homearts.com/depts/family/48stin21.htm> (November 21, 1998).

2. "Chatting Up a Storm on Halloween," <http://www.scholastic.com/goosebumps/high/stine/chat.htm> (November 21, 1998).

3. Ibid.

4. R. L. Stine, as told to Joe Arthur, *It Came From Ohio* (New York: Scholastic, 1997), p. 7.

5. "R. L. Stine," <http://www.homearts.com/depts/family/48stin21.htm>.

6. "Chatting Up a Storm on Halloween."

7. *Biography Today* (New York: H. W. Wilson, 1994), p. 318.

8. Stine, p. 84.

9. Ibid., p. 97.

10. Ibid., p. 101.

11. "Chatting Up a Storm on Halloween."

12. Stine, p. 112.

13. *Biography Today*, p. 320.

14. "Chatting Up a Storm on Halloween."

15. "R. L. Stine," <http://www.homearts.com/depts/family/48stin51.htm>.

16. "Chatting Up a Storm on Halloween."

17. M. Silver, "Horrors! It's R. L. Stine!" *U.S. News and World Report*, October 23, 1995, p. 96.

Chapter 10. Laurence Yep

1. Laurence Yep, *The Lost Garden* (Englewood Cliffs, N.J.: Julian Messner, 1991), p. 41.

2. *Something About the Author* (Detroit: Gale, 1992), vol. 69, p. 231.

3. *Asian American Biography* (New York: UXL, 1995), vol. 2, p. 391.

4. Patrick Burnson, "In the Studio with Laurence Yep," *Publishers Weekly*, May 16, 1994, p. 25.

5. Yep, p. 91.

6. Ibid.

7. Ibid., p. 95.

8. Alleen P. Nilsen, ed., *Literature for Today's Young Adults* (New York: HarperCollins, 1993), p. 233.

9. Dianne Johnson-Feelings, *Presenting Laurence Yep* (New York: Twayne, 1995), p. 107.

10. Yep, p. 5.

11. *Something About the Author*, p. 233.

12. Johnson-Feelings, p. 11.

13. Nilsen, p. 223.

14. Ibid., p. 102.

15. *Something About the Author* (Detroit: Gale, 1991), vol. 65, p. 184.

16. Burnson, p. 26.

Further Reading

A Selected List

Ehrlich, Amy, ed. *When I Was Your Age*. Cambridge, Mass.: Candlewick Press, 1996.

Kay Vandergrift's Young Adult Literature Page: <http://www.scils.rutgers.edu/special/kay/yalit.html>

Yunghans, Penelope. *Prize Winners: Ten Writers for Young Readers*. Greensboro, N.C.: Morgan Reynolds, 1995.

• • •

By Judy Blume

The One in the Middle Is the Green Kangaroo, 1969
Iggie's House, 1970
Are You There God? It's Me, Margaret, 1970
Tales of a Fourth Grade Nothing, 1972
Otherwise Known As Sheila the Great, 1972
Blubber, 1974
Forever, 1975
Starring Sally J. Freedman As Herself, 1977
Tiger Eyes, 1981
Letters to Judy, 1986
Just As Long As We're Together, 1987
Here's to You, Rachel Robinson, 1993

About Judy Blume

Blume, Judy. *Letters to Judy*. New York: Putnam, 1986.
Current Biography. New York: H. W. Wilson, 1980.
Lee, Betsy. *Judy Blume's Story*. Minneapolis: Dillon, 1981.
Something About the Author. Volume 79. Detroit: Gale, 1995.

Weidt, Maryann N. *Presenting Judy Blume.* Boston: Twayne, 1990.

"Judy Blume Homepage," <http://www.judyblume.com>

• • •

By Virginia Hamilton

Zeely, 1967
The House of Dies Drear, 1969
The Planet of Junior Brown, 1971
M. C. Higgins the Great, 1974
Sweet Whispers, Brother Rush, 1982
Willie Bea and the Time the Martians Landed, 1983
In the Beginning, 1988
Cousins, 1990
Plain City, 1993
Second Cousins, 1998
Bluish, 1999

About Virginia Hamilton

Contemporary Authors, New Revision. Volume 20. Detroit: Gale, 1987.

Mikkelsen, Nina. *Virginia Hamilton.* New York: Twayne, 1994.

Something About the Author. Volume 79. Detroit: Gale, 1995.

"Virginia Hamilton Homepage."
<http://www.virginiahamilton.com>

• • •

By Julius Lester

To Be a Slave, 1969
The Long Journey Home, 1972
Two Love Stories, 1972
This Strange New Feeling, 1982

Othello, 1995
From Slave Ship to Freedom Road, 1998
Pharaoh's Daughter, 2000

About Julius Lester

Contemporary Black Biography. Volume 9. Detroit: Gale, 1995.
Lester, Julius. *Lovesong.* New York: Arcade, 1988.
Something About the Author. Volume 74. Detroit: Gale, 1993.
"Julius Lester."
<http://www.indiana.edu/~eric_rec/ieo/bibs/lester.html>

• • •

By Lois Lowry

A Summer to Die, 1977
Autumn Street, 1979
Anastasia Krupnik, 1979
All About Sam, 1988
Number the Stars, 1989
The Giver, 1993
Looking Back, 1998

About Lois Lowry

Chaston, Joel D. *Lois Lowry.* New York: Twayne, 1997.
Lowry, Lois. *Looking Back.* Boston: Houghton Mifflin, 1998.
Markham, Lois. *Lois Lowry.* Santa Barbara: Learning Works, 1995.
Something About the Author: Autobiography Series. Volume 3. Detroit: Gale, 1987.
A Visit With Lois Lowry (videocassette). Boston: Houghton Mifflin, 1985.

"Ask the Author: Lois Lowry."
<http://www.ipl.org/youth/AskAuthor/Lowry.html>

• • •

By Phyllis Reynolds Naylor

The Galloping Goat and Other Stories, 1965
What the Gulls Were Singing, 1967
How I Came to Be a Writer, 1978
The Agony of Alice, 1985
Shiloh, 1991
Shiloh Season, 1996
Saving Shiloh, 1997
Walker's Crossing, 1999

About Phyllis Reynolds Naylor

Naylor, Phyllis Reynolds. *How I Came to Be a Writer.* New York: Atheneum, 1978.

Something About the Author. Volume 102. Detroit: Gale, 1998.

Something About the Author: Autobiography Series. Volume 10. Detroit: Gale, 1990.

Stover, Thomas. *Presenting Phyllis Reynolds Naylor.* New York: Twayne, 1997.

Internet Public Library Youth Division: Ask the Author, "Phyllis Reynolds Naylor."

<http://www.ipl.org/youth/AskAuthor/Naylor.html>

The Alice Fan Club.

<http://www.simonsays.com/kids/alice/index.cfm>

• • •

By Katherine Paterson

The Sign of the Chrysanthemum, 1973
Of Nightingales That Weep, 1974

The Master Puppeteer, 1976
Bridge to Terabithia, 1977
The Great Gilly Hopkins, 1978
Jacob Have I Loved, 1980
Lyddie, 1991
Jip: His Story, 1996
Preacher's Boy, 1999

About Katherine Paterson

Cary, Alice. *Katherine Paterson*. Santa Barbara, Calif.: Learning Works, 1997.
Current Biography. New York: H. W. Wilson, 1997.
Paterson, Katherine. *A Sense of Wonder*. New York: Plume, 1995.
Schmidt, Gary D. *Katherine Paterson*. New York: Twayne, 1994.
Something About the Author. Volume 92. Detroit: Gale, 1997.
"Ask the Author: Katherine Paterson."
<http://www.ipl.org/youth/AskAuthor/paterson.html>
Katherine Paterson Homepage.
<http://www.terabithia.com>

• • •

By Gary Paulsen

Popcorn Days and Buttermilk Nights, 1983
Dancing Carl, 1983
Dogsong, 1985
Hatchet, 1987
The Winter Room, 1989
Canyons, 1990
Woodsong, 1990
The River, 1991
Nightjohn, 1993

Brian's Winter, 1996
Brian's Return, 1999

About Gary Paulsen

Paulsen, Gary. *Woodsong*. New York: Simon & Schuster, 1990.

Salvner, Gary M. *Presenting Gary Paulsen*. New York: Twayne, 1996.

Something About the Author. Volume 79. Detroit: Gale, 1995.

Gary Paulsen Homepage. <http://www.garypaulsen.com>

• • •

By Gary Soto

Living Up the Street, 1985
Baseball in April and Other Stories, 1990
Taking Sides, 1991
A Fire in My Hand, 1991
Pacific Crossing, 1992
Neighborhood Odes, 1992
Canto Familiar, 1995
Jesse, 1995
Buried Onions, 1997
Nerdlandia, 1999

About Gary Soto

Contemporary Authors. Volume 125. Detroit: Gale, 1989.

Dictionary of Literary Biography. Volume 82. Detroit: Gale, 1989.

Something About the Author. Volume 80. Detroit: Gale, 1995.

Soto, Gary. *Living Up the Street*. New York: Dell, 1985.

The Official Gary Soto Website.
<http://www.garysoto.com>

By R. L. Stine

How to Be Funny, 1978
Blind Date, 1986
The New Girl (Fear Street #1), 1989
Welcome to Dead House (Goosebumps #1), 1992
The Cry of the Cat (Goosebumps Series 2000 #1), 1998
Nightmare Hour, 1999

About R. L. Stine

Jones, Patrick. *What's So Scary About R. L. Stine?* Lanham, Md.: Scarecrow Press, 1998.
Biography Today. New York: H. W. Wilson, 1994.
Something About the Author. Volume 76. Detroit: Gale, 1994.
Stine, R. L., as told to Joe Arthur. *It Came From Ohio: My Life As a Writer*. New York: Scholastic, 1997
Fear Street Home Page. <http://www.fearstreet.com>

Goosebumps Home Page.
<http://www.scholastic.com/goosebumps>

• • •

By Laurence Yep

Sweetwater, 1973
Dragonwings, 1975
Child of the Owl, 1977
Sea Glass, 1979
The Lost Garden, 1991
Dragon's Gate, 1993
The Amah, 1999

About Laurence Yep

Asian American Biography. Volume 2. New York: UXL, 1995.

Johnson-Feelings, Dianne. *Presenting Laurence Yep.* New York: Twayne, 1995.

Something About the Author. Volume 69. Detroit: Gale, 1992.

Yep, Laurence. *The Lost Garden.* Englewood Cliffs, N.J.: Julian Messner, 1991.

"Laurence Yep."
<http://www.scils.rutgers.edu/special/kay/yep.html>

Index

Numbers in boldface type indicate photographs.